101 Things You H
in a Wheelchair

Jacket design by Ken Reid and Michael Offutt
Edited by Michael Offutt

This book is dedicated to my loving family

Contents

101 Things You Have Wondered about Someone in a Wheelchair...9

  Introduction 11

  Chapter 1 13

    1. What were your first thoughts after waking up from your accident?...13

    2. What was it like not being able to move your legs?...14

    3. Did you cry? 15

    4. Were you mad?...16

    5. Did I want to die? 16

    6. Were you scared? 17

    7. Did you blame yourself? 18

    8. Do you dream about walking?..............................19

    9. When did you realize it was permanent?...................20

    10. How much pain were you in? 21

  On the Lighter Side! 23

  Chapter 2 24

    11. How do you get dressed?...................................24

    12. How do you go to the bathroom? 25

    13. How did it make you feel knowing you had to do this for the rest of your life? 28

    14. How did you learn to transfer? 29

    15. Did you ever want to quit? 30

    16. Did it hurt doing rehab?....................................31

    17. What type of exercises did you do?.......................31

    18. Did you have someone that helped you or that you learned from?...32

    19. What was your best moments and worse moments of rehab? 34

    20. How did you learn how to drive? 35

  On the Lighter Side 2 37

  Chapter 3 39

    21. What was it like going home? 39

    22. Do you sleep in a regular bed? 39

    23. What modifications to your home did you have to do? 40

    24. When did you go back to work?...........................41

    25. After you got home did you get depressed? 42

26. Did you do more rehab after you got home?............42

27. Do you stay in your wheelchair when watching
television?...43

28. Was your wife sad? 43

29. Was your family sad? 44

30. What kept you sane after losing all that you had?....44

On the Lighter Side 3 47

Chapter 4 48

31. Can you still have sex? 50

32. Can you orgasm? 51

33. How is sex different?..51

34. Do you still desire sex?..51

35. Can you still get an erection? 52

36. Can you ejaculate?..53

37. Can you still be spontaneous? 53

38. Were you afraid to make love the first time after you
were paralyzed? 54

39. Do you still feel sexy or wanted? 54

40. Can you still get into different positions?................55

On the Lighter Side 4 57

Chapter 5 58

41. Do you still play sports?...58

42. When did you start bowling again? 59

43. What tournaments have you won since being in the
wheelchair?..59

44. Did you ever win a professional bowler's
tournament? 60

45. Do you use different chairs for sports?....................60

46. How many wheelchairs do you have? 61

47. Do you bowl in a wheelchair bowling league? 63

48. Do you travel to sports tournaments?......................64

49. How is it to fly with your wheelchair? 65

50. Has the airlines ever lost your chair? 67

On the Lighter Side 5! 68

Chapter 6 69

51. Have you ever fallen out of your wheelchair?..........69

52. Have you ever fallen in the shower? 70

53. Do you do dishes? 71

54. Do you vacuum?..72

55. Do you do the wash? 72

56. Do you clean the bathroom?....................................72

57. Do you do windows?..73

58. Do you do the lawn?...73

59. Do you do the garden?...73

60. Do you work on your own car? 73

On the Lighter Side 6 75

Chapter 7 76

61. What is a pressure sore and how do they happen? ...76

62. Have you ever broken a bone? 77

63. What is a U.T.I.?..77

64. Why does your leg shake?.......................................78

65. How come you can't cough? 78

66. Have you been in the hospital since your accident?.79

67. How can you tolerate hospital food? 79

68. Do you get sicker now? 80

69. Why do you hold your legs?....................................81

70. Do you have pain now? 82

On the Lighter Side 7 83

Chapter 8 84

71. How much did your most expensive wheelchair cost?

....84

72. What do you do in case of a flat tire? 84

73. Why don't you use a power wheelchair instead of a

manual wheelchair? 85

74. What is the longest wheelie you have done?............87

75. Can you go down steps in your chair?.....................87

76. Can you go upstairs? 88

77. Can you jump ramps?..88

78. Have you ever gotten into a fight in your wheelchair?

....89

79. Has your wheel ever fallen off your wheelchair?.....90

80. How do you reach cabinets while in your wheelchair?

....92

On the Lighter Side 8 93

Chapter 9 94

81. Do you go on roller coasters?..................................94

82. Are most restaurants accessible? 95

83. Do you know when you are hungry?........................96

84. Do you know when you are full? 96

85. Do you get mad when an able-bodied person parks in

a handicapped parking space? 97
86. What do you do if there is not a ramp? 98
87. How do you go shopping?..99
88. Since the A.D.A. is there someplace you want to go
but can't? 100
89. How do you feel when someone asks you if you need
help? 100
90. Why do you usually refuse help? 101
On the Lighter Side 9 102
The Future 104
91. What would you do if a fire happened in your home?
....104
92. How do you feel about medical marijuana? 105
93. How do you feel about stem cell treatments?.........105
94. Would you get the operation?.................................107
95. If you were to get the operation and everything went
perfect what would be the first thing you would do? ...108
96. When did you start speaking?.................................109
97. When you are speaking are you scared?.................110
98. How did you feel the first time you got a standing
ovation? 111
99. How do you feel about signing autographs? 112
100. How much speaking do you want to do?..............112
101. Do you feel you're happier now than when you were
able-bodied? 114
About the Author...115

101 Things You Have Wondered about Someone in a Wheelchair

By Ken Reid

Introduction

I wrote this book due to all the questions I have gotten through the twenty plus years of being in a wheelchair. I can't express enough thanks for the contributions I have received from friends and other wheelchair users in helping me finish this book. In between each chapter I have included funny stories from me and other wheelchair users that I hope you will enjoy!

Chapter 1

1. What were your first thoughts after waking up from your accident?

For me it was like "Oh my God what have I done?" I had seen those familiar lights above my head, I knew it wasn't good. It was very confusing and scary at the same time. I tried my hardest to remember what had happened but could not remember a thing. I remember seeing my mom, dad, and my wife with tears in their eyes as they tried explaining the car accident. I was still in a medically induced state, so everything seemed foggy.

For others this is a terrible time as they come to realize exactly what has happened. For me it was very hard just trying to connect the dots. Thoughts raced through my head about what had happened, trying to put a puzzle together that had no pieces that connected. I remembered thinking I don't feel no pain now besides a slight headache. It was hard just trying to keep my eyes open let alone comprehend anything that was being said. I drifted in and out of sleep trying to make sense of it all. When I would wake up again, I would think about: *who was driving? where were we at? what caused the wreck? did anyone die? oh my god did I kill someone? or is someone hurt badly because of me?* All these thoughts came to me as I laid there in the hospital bed.

Eventually I would learn that I was in a car accident, but no one had died. A friend of mine and I were coming back from bowling. We were both professional bowlers on the Professional Bowlers Tour and had gotten into an accident. I was not driving but I did not have my seat belt on and was thrown from the car. My friend survived the wreck because he was wearing his seat belt. He was driving a 1987 Corvette and had taken it up to one-hundred miles per hour. He couldn't make the curve in the road at that speed, and he lost control of it after hitting a ditch. I flew out of the vehicle and landed in a ditch a hundred-fifty feet from the car. I suffered internal injuries and was ultimately paralyzed because of this.

2. What was it like not being able to move your legs?

When I was able to finally comprehend all the things that were being said to me, that's when I realized that I could not move my legs. Fright and anxiety and sheer terror quickly took over my mind and body. I tried my hardest to move my legs to prove them wrong, but it felt like my legs were in concrete and were not moving at all. To have a part of your body not move when you are sending a message to it *to move* is very nerve wracking to say the least! It was then that I heard that word I could not believe I was hearing: "PARALYZED!"

Again, thoughts raced through my head: *is it*

permanent? will I ever be able to walk again? what about kids? how do I go to the bathroom? The sheer terror of hearing that word still haunts me to this day. I think parents of a child born with a disability go through the same thing when they hear "whatever it is" named by the doctor for the first time. Spina bifida, cerebral palsy, and muscular dystrophy, just to name a few are the words that any parent dreads to hear when they are having a child. They know the life ahead will be very difficult for them and their child. My parents and wife were no different regarding the word, "paralyzed." I'm sure it had the same effect on them.

3. Did you cry?

Like a baby! There were so many times that I broke down crying—I'm sure I could not count that high on both of my hands! I don't think I was so much distraught because of paralysis. Rather, it was because of what I'd perceived that I'd lost. It was about how I'd screwed up not only my life, but the lives of my family, friends and even co-workers. It affected everyone that knew me, and (as time would show) it even influenced everyone that I'd meet.

I found out this was the good thing about showers: you could cry as much as you wanted in them and no one could tell! Depression is a very real thing with a disability and knowing that you will need a wheelchair the rest of your life can deal a very hard blow to whomever finds out they'll need to rely upon one for their mobility. Knowing that there are others out there already that have proven that just because you're in a wheelchair does not mean that life is over. It's learning to accept that life has just changed. You can change and adapt to a new world from a wheelchair. It might not be easy, but it can still be very rewarding.

4. Were you mad?

This is a hard one to answer as I was very mad, not at the reason why it happened, or even how it happened, but that *I let it happen*. Both I and the driver were drinking that night, and it was nothing that we hadn't done many times before. Looking back on the event, I think it was just a matter of time before something bad happened. I have no hard feelings against my friend who was driving, and who was ultimately responsible for the accident. If I should be mad at anyone it should be me. I'm the one that got too drunk to know what I was doing, and I'm the one who told my friend to go for it when he asked if he could take the car up to a hundred miles per hour. Yes, we must take accountability for our actions and this one was just as much my fault as it was my friends. I was mad at God as I could not understand how he could let this happen. But in time I would realize it wasn't God that did this, or my friend. No, it was me that did this. It was my decision that put me in that position.

5. Did I want to die?

I must be truthful, there were times I did wish I would have died in the car accident. Not because I felt sorry for myself, but because I really didn't want to go through all the rehabilitation and live my life like this. Sometimes when we are faced with life's challenges only then will we know our full capabilities. Looking back now, I can see how selfish that would have been. The accident didn't just affect me but everyone I knew. Although I had loss, if I would have died, there would have been so many others who would have felt grief for the rest of their lives. No, I knew I had to face this challenge on my own for better or worse. This was all my doing and it was up to me to make the most of my new life in the wheelchair. As I laid there in that bed, I realized that I survived the car accident for some reason. It was up to me to find the reason. Death was not an alternative to me, and I am very much against suicide and would never even consider it. There was a lot of soul-searching that needed to be done, and I'll say from experience that when you can't move or get out of the bed on your own you suddenly have a lot more time on your hands.

6. Were you scared?

Yes, yes, yes! I feared the unknown! You're being given a lot of information all at one time. Trying to make sense of it all is a daunting thing. Dealing with the accident itself and then thinking about what your future will hold is very scary. Although I had family and friends by my side, I still felt all alone! I felt numb, like it wasn't real, but I would wake up the next day and reality would sink in once again with a voice whispering, "You are permanently paralyzed, Ken."

I liken it to riding a roller coaster of emotions. One minute you'd be up and feeling great, and in the next moment, the depression demons would show their ugly face again. You think of your life, how it was, how you pray things will change, and yet…they don't. That's when you think to yourself, "How am I going to be able to carry on?"

Call it pure faith (or whatever you want) but the human spirit inside has an incredible urge to continue. Being scared is not shameful as it shows the true emotion you have inside, being able to harness the fright and using that emotion to make it into a positive force for good is the true challenge! We all must be able to face our fears whether it's just a simple fear or a major one, having the courage and will to continue is a feature the human spirit possesses. Use it to your advantage whenever you can. You never know what you're capable of until you overcome that fear!

7. Did you blame yourself?

I blamed myself over and over for letting me get that drunk and for getting into that car knowing my friend had been drinking too. They say that hindsight is 20/20. Well, I can attest to that. The words: could of, would of, should of, have been thrown out of my vocabulary, because that kind of thinking is just water under the bridge. You can't keep beating yourself up over a mistake you've made. All you can do is try to learn from your mistakes and try your hardest not to duplicate them in the future.

I wasn't driving and I'm thankful for that. I'm also thankful that we did not kill anyone else in our accident. Yeah, I wasn't driving but I would've felt so incredibly bad if we had been the cause of taking another person's life due to our lack of judgment. Blame is a big word as it incriminates someone for something that they did against another. My buddy *didn't do this to me* and to blame him for something we had done many times before would be just unfair. No, I take as much responsibility if not more for my actions that fateful night and do not blame my buddy for me being confined to a wheelchair the rest of my life. It is pure freedom when you release someone from blame and tell them it wasn't their fault. I truly believe that time heals all wounds and that we both will be better people because of it!

8. Do you dream about walking?

From time to time I dream about walking. Either it's a dream about bowling or walking on the beach or walking with my wife Vickie, but each one wakes me up with the reality of, "Yeah Ken, your still paralyzed." And then a whole new period of depression can be set off.

Fortunately, I'm different from others as I don't get depressed all that much. If I do, it doesn't last very long. I think to myself I have a lot to be thankful for, and it usually brings me out of it quick. However, I do experience incredible dreams of the way things used to be: the views from a standing position, the feel of sand between your toes, the feel of grass beneath your feet. They are all familiar feelings that I no longer get to experience.

So, dreams can be a double-edged sword as they can bring back happy feelings, but they can also bring back feelings of loss once again. I used to dream a lot when I was first paralyzed but as I age either I'm not remembering them, or they are not coming as frequently as before. So, I welcome dreams now as they are almost like a treat of the subconscious reminding me of the way things can still be if they do ever release the cure. I say "release the cure" cause they already have it, but it's just so caught up in bureaucracy and red tape it might not happen in my lifetime.

9. When did you realize it was permanent?

It took a while for it to sink in that I might not ever walk again. I say might not, because I still have hope that there will be a cure and that one-day people will not have to be confined to wheelchairs because of paralysis anymore. So, the word "permanent" basically is not a word I use unless it's to scream "I've been permanently healed!"

The realization that I will never walk again was a true blow to me and my faith. For example, how

20

could I not think, "Okay, God, your son died on the cross and you brought him back to life. The bible says you made a crippled man walk, a blind woman see, so why can't you fix me?"

They said I only bruised my spinal cord; I didn't sever it. Okay, so why can't I be fixed. Rather, why can't *He* fix me? These questions constantly go through my mind and shake my faith from time to time, but I just must come back to my beliefs and use my blind faith that he will heal me. However, I've got to realize that it might not be in my time but in His.

So, to answer the question I guess I realized that there was a possibility that I may never walk again right after I came off the morphine drip about six weeks after my car accident. Those were some tough words to hear…that your world has changed…and that your new reality is that *you are paralyzed.* And finally…that the complications of your paralysis are everlasting.

10. How much pain were you in?

Thankfully I was on a morphine drip as there was some major pain from all my injuries. I had suffered a closed head injury, broke all my ribs, lacerated my liver, broke my collar bone in four places, suffered a brachial plexus injury, and broke my back in the T4 thru T5 area. Other than that, I was fine. Just a couple of flesh wounds! ☺

As I came off the morphine drip my pain increased day by day. The brachial plexus is a group of nerve bundles that are located just below the shoulder area and they were the most active in my pain as I started feeling more and more of my body. I didn't have any pain in my lower extremities just throbs now and then pulsating through my numb legs. With all the other injuries I had, the medicine seemed to make it all bearable. Now that I was medicine free the pain would come in waves and all I could have now was Tylenol every four hours. Let's just say I became clock watcher down to the minute. But I knew I had to ween myself off the pain meds as that was the only way I was going to be able to start my rehabilitation. It was going to be an uphill climb all the way, but I knew there was only one way to go *and that was up*.

On the Lighter Side!

A quadriplegic friend of mine who uses a power wheelchair was walking his Great Dane service dog, Butch. He would attach the leash to his leg rest when taking him for a walk and drive his power wheelchair bedside him. Butch was a huge dog that looked really mean. He had a head on him that was as big as a football, very intimidating to say the least!

Well Butch was out for a walk when a little Chihuahua suddenly appeared around the corner. Butch got that look in his eye, and my buddy knew what was going to happen! You see…Butch was a big ole fraidy-cat and when he saw the little Chihuahua start racing toward him, he leaped in the air and landed in my friends lap in his wheelchair just a yelping as if he had just been shot by a gun! It was the funniest sight, seeing a two-hundred-pound dog in my friend's lap just trying to get away from the little ferocious dog!

Chapter 2

11. How do you get dressed?

Getting dressed is tough for a lot of people. There are a couple of ways to do it when you are in my situation. One is to get transferred into the bed and then use a rolling motion to work the pants. Basically, you alternate which side you pull them up on. For someone with limited hand function this is very difficult as loops will probably be needed to be sewn into the waist so they can hook the loop with their thumb or finger and work the pants up.

For paraplegics it's a little easier as they can get dressed in their chair reducing the amount of transfers and saving time. You would think that putting on a shirt would be easy, however trying to balance when you are in the bed is very difficult! That is why getting dressed in the chair is faster as you can use the back of the chair to help you balance.

For quadriplegics this is a very difficult thing as they sometimes must do it laying down. Just another obstacle in getting dressed to begin the day. Then we have the socks! Think about it, can you imagine how to stretch them out to get around your toes to even get the sock started? After that you must find a way to grip the sock's edge to pull them up. One tip is to cut a little hole about four inches down the sock to hook your thumb or finger through to lift the sock up the rest of the way. For paraplegics this is a little easier as they can grip with their fingers. Okay, we are almost through! Now comes the shoes.

One tip for the shoes are the retractable shoestrings—the type that coil up when put through the eye loops, so the shoe does not have to be tied. An even better one is the Velcro shoe straps—that way there *are no* shoelaces!

Believe it or not some quadriplegics can get completely dressed by themselves within ten minutes. It takes technique, practice, and just being able to think through complications you might encounter, to get ready every day. "What complications?" you might ask? Well, what if you drop a sock or shoe off the bed and must get transferred back in your chair just to pick up the shoe or sock *and then* get transferred back into bed to finish putting them on. Sometimes getting dressed can take as much as a half an hour. Heck, after an ordeal like that some of you might be ready to get back into bed and go to sleep! ☺

12. How do you go to the bathroom?

This might be a gross answer so proceed with caution! This can be a very difficult time in a disabled person's life. Most people don't realize the difficulty someone that is in a wheelchair must go through. You see, this is the most unwanted thing a person in a wheelchair must do. For a paraplegic we usually use a suppository that helps our stool come out, and sometimes it can take some time for the

25

suppository to work. Sometimes it works in as little as fifteen minutes, and on other occasions it can take up to forty-five minutes to get things moving.

There are other suppositories that sometimes work faster, but they aren't reliably fast every time you use them. In any event, once the stool starts to move, we must then do a manual check to see if all of it has come out. This is done with a rubber glove and inserting a finger in the rectum. Then, and using a circular motion, you stimulate the anus to see if there is any more stool that needs to come out. By doing this you verify that the lower tract of the bowel is empty. And what happens if you did not get it fully emptied? You guessed it. You have a bowel movement later in the day right in your pants that you now must get cleaned up. So, if you're at work…this means you transfer back into your car, you drive home, get transferred back into your chair, transfer into your shower chair in the bathroom, take off your soiled clothes, and *all of this is done while getting stuff all over you*. Then you grab your cushion, take the cover off, wash the bottom and wipe down the cushion (as a side note, this is why incontinent covers are worth the price), and then we start the process of cleaning up the mess we have on our body!

If you took the time to read all of that, you can see why this is the most unpleasant and unwanted part of being in a wheelchair! Now, you might wonder to yourself, "Well how does someone with no hand function do that?" The answer is that it's very difficult and rare for a quadriplegic who can do his bowel routine independently. Most have assistance to help them with their bowl care. For multiple sclerosis, spina bifida, cerebral palsy, muscular dystrophy, or anyone with limited hand movement (just to name a few) this is a daunting task they must do to get ready for the day. As you can see there is a lot more to being in the wheelchair than most people can see. But it's not all bad. Let me tell you about the easier thing: going pee.

On first consideration, you might think the act of peeing might be a lot easier, right? Not so fast. You see, this is where catheterization comes into play. What is catheterization you ask? Well it is when you take a thin tube and insert it into the urethra to allow elimination of urine out of the bladder. Seems like a simple concept, right? Well, actually…it's kinda complicated. When you are catheterizing yourself, you must be very careful not to get the catheter dirty. This requires you to wash your hands diligently, and to make sure the area is very clean. If these precautions are not carefully followed, you might get a urinary tract infection which can make you very sick and even cause death!

Lubrication must be used to allow the catheter to go in smoothly and not to cause any trauma to the urethra. Once inserted the urine can exit the bladder. Now for quadriplegics this can be almost impossible, so most people use a super pubic or indwelling catheter that is hooked to a leg bag that the bladder empties into. The catheter is inserted into the urethra and once it's in the bladder a small balloon the size of a dime is then filled with distilled water by using a syringe. This keeps the catheter from coming out. Yes, you can still get urinary infections as the catheter is a foreign object in the body that the body will try to expel if it can.

Anyway, as you can see, the bowl and bladder care are the most complicated, humiliating, dreaded, function that a person in a wheelchair must do. It seems sometimes that my life is run according to my bowel and bladder care. Trying to explain this to a boss or someone in charge or someone that just doesn't understand is very difficult as they might think you're taking advantage of your disability. Ha! Like you want to take advantage of your disability, sometimes I crack me up! No, fortunately I have a very understanding boss that knows regardless of what time I get to work I will put in my full eight hours or take personal leave to make up for it.

13. How did it make you feel knowing you had to do this for the rest of your life?

The realization that this will be a function and reoccurring event of your life every day is a very hard thing to swallow. Knowing that up to three hours a day will have to be set aside to do a bowel routine is almost like a death sentence but hey, how do you think I was able to write both my books? Yep, because I must stick my finger up my butt every day, I was able to take time to write my books. See Dad, you were wrong. I can get something done while sitting around with my finger up my ass! ☺

14. How did you learn to transfer?

A transfer is a technique that is used to move your body from one place to another. An example of a transfer is getting out of bed and into a wheelchair. Transferring is a very difficult and necessary thing for someone in a wheelchair to learn how to do. And there are certain techniques and movements one must learn to be able to transfer independently. If you've never tried before, take a dining room chair and place it by the couch. Now try to move your body from the couch to a dining room seat by not using your legs. I think it will be difficult for you, as you'll want to use your hamstrings to help with the transfer. However, for the experience to be as authentic as possible, I'd like you to try and not to use them and see how well you do! I'll go ahead and tell you that you'll be relying on your upper body strength alone.

The first thing you will notice is you will probably be able to lift yourself up into the air. But then you will need to get your upper body moving in the direction of the wheelchair. You can do this by leaning with your head to get your body started in the motion you will need to complete the transfer.

Please notice the muscles you use in generating the initial movement. Now imagine you being a quadriplegic or someone with weak upper body muscles. The placement of your hand put on the place where you wish to transfer will be key in making the transfer a success. If you lay your arm out too far, and it does not become a pivot point, then your transfer (more than likely) will not be successful. These techniques and movements must be learned before you can become independent in transfers.

Independence is what most everyone in the wheelchair strives for as you don't want someone doing something for you every day of your life when you can do it for yourself. However, people still ask me, "Are you too proud to be helped?" I simply tell them no, but I need to be able to do it by myself because there will come a time when there will be no one there to be able to help me. So, I must be independent in all my transfers for the time that I'm on my own.

15. Did you ever want to quit?

There were many times that I wanted to just quit because of the pain and exhaustion I would feel the next day because my muscles were so sore. I had been in ICU and the step-down unit for around eight weeks, so my muscles were so atrophied they had to be re-strengthened. This, on top of working out to get more strength to do the transfers, made rehabilitation very difficult. I was dealing with injuries that were still healing as well as a mental state of mind that was laser-focused on getting healthy enough to be able to be released to go home. And I want to reiterate that "going home" was the ultimate goal. It was my inspiration and fueled my drive to get out of rehab so that I could get back to real life and pick up the pieces of my life and start forging a new path.

16. Did it hurt doing rehab?

When I first started rehab there were only a few exercises I could do because of my right arm and the injury I had sustained to the arm and nerves in it. The brachial-plexus injury (deadening of the nerves to the arm), really caused a lot of pain and delays as to what I was able to do. There were many times when I would overdo it, and I ended up setting myself back a couple of days because I could barely move my right arm due to the pain. You know the feeling you get when your arm falls asleep and you feel the pins and needles sensation as it slowly wakes up? Well, that was what my arm felt like all the time as well as a very sore/pulled muscle in the same arm *at the same time*. So, you can see how pushing in a wheelchair or doing a push up or lifting weights was very difficult to do. Still I just told myself I had to work through the pain to get the results I wanted, and that was to go home!

17. What type of exercises did you do?

Although I was in pain most of the time, I tried to do all the exercises the physical therapist asked me to do. We would start in the morning around nine o'clock and work out in physical therapy.

There we would lift weights, but they were not the typical weight benches and machines as most people could only transfer onto a mat and then they would bring the weights over to us to start to lift.

I remember looking at a contraption that had two bicycle wheels with a bar going through the center of them with weights on the outside of the wheels. This was a makeshift bench press, as they would roll the wheels up to you and have them go on each side of you so that you could reach up and press the bar in the center the same way you would do it on a weight bench. Except (because of the wheels) there was no way of dropping the bar on your chest as the wheels would prevent it from getting close to your body.

Then there was the rickshaw machine. It was a machine where you backed your wheelchair into it, and it had two bars that came out on either side of your wheelchair. You would have weights placed on the back of these bars and then you'd need to push down on them to make the weights in the rear go up. This would help build your tricep muscles, the tricep muscle is the muscle that is on the back of your upper arm that helps you push down or lift your body up. This exercise is very important as (while you are sitting down) if you don't take the pressure off your buttocks, you could develop a pressure sore. A pressure sore is a deadening of skin due to lack of blood flow and oxygen. These sores are very dangerous and can even cause death.

18. Did you have someone that helped you

or that you learned from?

I had an incredible physical therapist named
Greta Nelson. She was a cute girl, but she was
tough as nails as my physical therapist. She knew
just the right buttons to push to get me mad enough
to make me want to do the task she was having me
do. And if I failed or missed a transfer or didn't do
it the way she wanted me to, I would hear the two
words I have grown to hate **"BOO HISSER!"**

She would say, "Ah boo hisser, is that the best
you can do girly man?"

And that was it. I would get so pissed off that I
could do just about anything she asked when I heard
those words! I also met the most inspirational
quadriplegic named Dusty Wheeler, (and yes that
was his name), who showed me how to make the
most out of my time there in rehab. You see, Dusty
only weighed around one-hundred pounds soaking
wet but could do most all the transfers perfectly due
to his technique and determination. It was amazing
watching him do the transfers like poetry in motion.
He had the perfect build as he was only around five-
foot two inches tall, but he was able to use his
height and weight to his advantage to help make his
transfers.

I watched Dusty very closely as he would lead
with his head when transferring, which would
lessen the weight on his bottom this would allow
him to get his body into motion by using his upper
body as weight. Even though he had no hand
function he was able to use his wrist and forearm as
a pivot point and pivot his body to where he wanted

to go. Greta said Dusty was like a super quad as he was able to transfer as good if not better than most paraplegics. I can't thank him enough for taking the time to help me get to be independent in my transfers.

Greta would work me out and just about kill me and then Dusty would not let me stop until I pushed a mile in my chair after dinner. There was an area in the middle of the rehab center that was outside and if you went around the compound four times it equaled one mile. Dusty would always do it after dinner to complete his workout for the day. He was a slave driver, but he got me thinking in the right frame of mind: I needed to do extra to help me get stronger to get out of rehab.

19. What was your best moments and worse moments of rehab?

The worst moments of rehab had to be the inability to do the required exercises and strengthening because of the pain I had in my right arm. I felt like people thought I was just using it as an excuse, if they only knew of how bad I wanted to get out of there and get on with my life. Most of the time I just worked through the pain—my eye was on the goal of getting out of rehab. The best was (by far) meeting the most inspirational people I have ever met. We were all in there together and the camaraderie was just unbelievable. I made friends there that I will never forget. It was hard watching others succeed while I did not, moving on to another task or transfer, but each time it was like a small victory we were all able to participate in.

20. How did you learn how to drive?

My Rehabilitation center was in the Blue Ridge Mountains of Virginia. We learned to drive around the campus, and when we completed the training there, we had to go out onto the main roads which led through the mountains. Let's just say you learn very fast on how to control the car and white-knuckle the steering wheel the whole way around those mountain passes.

There are different types of hand controls to help individuals drive without the use of their legs. For a paraplegic or someone that has the ability to grip a steering knob, all they really need is a steering spinner knob, (a knob that is attached to the steering wheel that allows you to turn the steering wheel with one hand), and a lever that is attached to the brake and the accelerator to control braking and acceleration.

Most of the hand controls are "pull down" to accelerate and "push in" to brake. For a quadriplegic that does not have the ability to grip a steering knob they might use a tri-pin steering apparatus in which they would put their hand into it. By using their wrist, the tri-pin cradle would spin like a spinner knob and enable the steering wheel to be turned. Then for the accelerator, they would use the same type of apparatus that would be attached to the brake and accelerator.

In 2019, there are many different types of hand controls, and they should be spec'd out by a professional.

On the Lighter Side 2

I had gone out to the mall to do some shopping and was in a bit of a hurry to get the items I needed and get back home quickly. One of the biggest downfalls of being in a wheelchair is you must catheterize yourself at set times to keep the bladder on a so-called schedule. This helps to prevent any unexpected accidents.

Well I'm rolling through the mall at a pretty fast pace and realize it's that time of the day that I need to go to the bathroom. So, I find the nearest bathroom and do my business and wash my hands and head out the door. The bathrooms in the mall were in the food court, so I come flying out of the bathroom to a very crowded food court and start making my way to the elevator to finish getting my items that I needed. While pushing through the crowded food court, a man in overalls (he looked like a farmer) tries to stop me and he says, "Whoa whoa whoa there buddy, the horse is still out of the barn!"

I'm thinking to myself *whatever Mr. Greenjeans I've got to go!* So, I blow by him trying to catch the elevator to go downstairs, and I just make it in the doors before they close. Now out of breath, I notice two guys in the elevator that held the door for me. They both look at each other and make startled looks and then the one closest to me leans over and whispers, "Dude, I think you forgot to put something away!"

That's when I looked down and noticed that my

manhood was totally exposed as I forgot to put it back in my pants when I finished cathing! You can only imagine the embarrassment I felt knowing that I had just gone through the whole food court with everything hanging out for all the world to see! Me and both the two guys in the elevator just busted out laughing when I told them where I had just come from!

Chapter 3

21. What was it like going home?

For those that have had a traumatic accident like I had, returning home is a time that is full of a lot of different emotions. You're excited to finally be able to return home, but there is also: fear of the unknown, adjusting to life in the wheelchair, coming to reality that this has happened, and this is *now* the rest of your life.

For most people, their homes are not made for a wheelchair, so they must have it modified to allow a wheelchair to go through the doorways and hallways. So, here's another layer of stress and helplessness as many are overwhelmed as to what must be done to make the home accessible for someone in a wheelchair.

And then there's the depression and anxiety as a result of what has happened, what was lost, and what might never happen again. However, I at least had a silver-lining: I was excited to show the world what I'm still capable of and to prove to myself that I can live a most productive life and still function as any other man would or could.

22. Do you sleep in a regular bed?

Fortunately, I can independently get in and out

of bed by myself. Other people with different disabilities must rely on someone else to assist with getting in and out of bed. For example, those with limited muscle tone might have to use a hospital-type bed to help raise and lower the head of the bed or the foot of the bed. Some beds even can raise up and down to help with transfers. If you are not able to roll over at night or readjust your body, you might have to use an alternate pressure relieving mattress.

This is a mattress that has chambers that inflate and deflate causing a rolling type motion which helps to reduce pressure. When someone cannot readjust themselves, their bodies are susceptible to pressure ulcers or sores from constant pressure on a bony area. If the pressure is not relieved or reduced the person can develop a bed sore which can be very hard to heal. I can toss and turn at night so I'm lucky that I don't have to have an adjustable air mattress. I do use a sheepskin pad on my ankles as the boney areas of my ankles tend to get red a lot, meaning they are not getting enough pressure relief.

23. What modifications to your home did you have to do?

As I stated earlier most homes are not wheelchair-friendly, meaning there are often steps or obstacles preventing access with a wheelchair. Most common are the bathrooms and access into and out of the home. When I first moved here to Utah in 2000, we rented an apartment that was already wheelchair accessible. We had the ability to build our own home after being in the apartment for two years. We made the bathrooms bigger and the closets bigger and built a rambler style home to eliminate steps. If you are not fortunate enough to build your own home and must modify your existing home, here are some tips:

1. Try to do a pocket door that recesses into the wall to eliminate door swing.
2. If a doorway is just a little too narrow for access, try some recessed hinges. These might be able to get you a couple more inches of clearance.
3. For bathing, a roll-in shower is usually the best. However (and in case this is not an option) using a transfer shower bench might be the best way to go.

24. When did you go back to work?

When I got hurt, my place of employment was on the second floor with no elevator in the building. This was back in 1990, and I didn't want to put any hardship on my former employer to have access built for me. So, I never went back to work where I was employed. So many people apply for Social Security Disability and Medicaid and get caught in a catch 22 situation where they don't want to go to work and lose all their benefits.

The problem with that scenario is they'll probably live in that same situation the rest of their lives. I didn't want to be in that situation, not that people who do can't lead happy lives. Rather, I knew I could still work and wanted to have a family and be able to provide for them. So, with a small insurance settlement of $25,000 dollars, I started my own durable medical equipment shop selling wheelchairs and medical supplies. It was a financial success, and I owned it for nine years before moving here to Utah.

25. After you got home did you get depressed?

For many people who get home from being in the hospital and begin a routine that starts to resemble something *this side of normal*...well, that's when the depression can set in. I'm not going to say I wasn't or didn't get depressed, but mine came in waves. It was usually brought on by something that didn't go right either because of a missed transfer or coming down with a urinary tract infection (U.T.I.) or a pressure sore—anything really that forced me to marinate in all the negative thoughts regarding activities I could no longer do.

26. Did you do more rehab after you got home?

When I first went home, me and my wife had to move in with my parents. The townhouse I was living in was totally not wheelchair accessible, so me and my wife had to move back in with my parents until we found a more accessible place. Luckily for me my brothers were still living at home, and they were very much into weightlifting. They were pretty brutal on me (like Greta, my former physical therapist, used to be). I thought I got away from the difficult physical therapy, but once again I was wrong! My brothers set up a workout schedule and would not let me stray from their workout times. So yes, I did do more rehab. It was not by choice, but it was well worth it in the end as I became stronger with the help of my brothers!

27. Do you stay in your wheelchair when watching television?

Whenever I can get out of my wheelchair I do. I like to feel normal at times like I'm like everyone else and just get away from the jail I call my wheelchair! Getting the transfer from the wheelchair to the couch and back from the couch to the wheelchair was difficult at first, but once I got the technique down it became second nature to me.

28. Was your wife sad?

After me and my wife got home things changed. The tragedy took a toll on our relationship, and we moved into a friendship area. I'd describe it as kinda like the friends *without benefits* type of scenario…if you get my drift. The accident affected so much more than just me and unfortunately it affected her the most. My parents arranged her to be able to stay with me through all my rehab, and I cannot thank her enough for helping me get through it. Eventually we grew apart. So much so that we ended our marriage a year after returning home.

29. Was your family sad?

My family was very supportive, and they were sad, but I think the fact I had survived the accident and was returning to somewhat of my old self seemed to help them. They were really worried about me when my marriage ended. I assured them that I had been through the toughest moments in my life and I was going to continue and that there was someone special out there I was supposed to meet!

I think one of the things they were saddest about was that I was not independent and on my own anymore. They wanted me to have my own life and be successful and right now at this moment it was hard to see the light at the end of the tunnel. But I assured them that I had just been through the toughest time in my life and that if I could survive that I would be up for anything. It was funny because the roles had changed. Instead of them being the positive enforcers it was me now trying to make them comfortable with the changes life had wrought.

30. What kept you sane after losing all that you had?

I got to tell you this was a lot tougher than I ever thought it would ever be. Losing someone you thought loved you as much as you loved her is a big blow to the self-esteem. Now, not only had I lost my job, my apartment, my bowling career, but now I had lost my wife and was living at home with my parents. I had officially hit rock bottom! I had a huge faith in God but felt he was not helping me at this time in my life. I asked, "Why have you forsaken me?" And I recalled when Jesus was on the cross asking the same thing. And I thought about how life and history played out and if things didn't happen, we would not be where we are now.

But still it's hard to accept when you're lying in that bed feeling sorry for yourself for anything to help. Well I knew I had been given a second chance but for what? Was this the plan to let me realize that because of a stupid mistake I had made I was going to be paralyzed and living with my parents the rest of my life? Well I told myself this is not what I want, and I'm against suicide so the only thing left was to pick my disabled butt up, tough it out, and make the best life that I can with what I have left. And that's exactly what I did! I started lifting weights, got back into shape, and went on with my life! There were so many other people in chairs that were living incredible lives, and I told myself I was going to be one of them. Eventually I would meet another woman, and it wasn't because she felt sorry for me. It was because I didn't let my accident take my life.

Instead, I made a life despite it!

On the Lighter Side 3

If you didn't know this already, chocolate is a natural laxative.

So, most disabled people try to stay away from it as much as they can. I (for one) am a chocoholic, and this does not go well with a disability or someone that does not have control of their bowels.

One day, a good friend of mine who was a quadriplegic was unaware of this little bit of information! It was Easter and like a lot of people, he got candy and a huge chocolate bunny. Well my buddy was a chocoholic as well, but he was newly injured and had no idea of the characteristics or side effects of chocolate. Well the day after Easter my buddy calls me up and said the Easter Bunny had revisited him last night.

I said, "What are you talking about?"

And he proceeded to tell me that when he went to sleep that night he usually sleeps on his side. He then added that he was sleeping as he usually does, and he had a bowel movement through the night. Now (and as you now know) being a quadriplegic makes it difficult to get out of bed. So, he called in his mom and when she went to help clean him up, she pulled back the covers. Because of the way he sleeps on his side, his movement was shaped perfectly like an Easter bunny. His mom could not hold back her laughter as she said he pooped it out whole! The two of them just laughed making a very uncomfortable situation bearable!

Chapter 4

For the people who know me and know how long the book has taken me to finish, this next chapter is the true reason why. You see me and my wife, Vickie, had read books about spinal cord injured individuals and even other disability books and one thing we both noticed was that there was very little information out there regarding sex.

Well I'm here to tell you that yes, the disabled have sex. And yes, it is very enjoyable and yes, some can even experience orgasm and total sexual fulfillment!

Some of this chapter will be about some of our experiences, and some will be from people who contributed to this book. I must thank those that shared their intimate experiences, and I thank you so much for not thinking I was a pervert! ☺

First and foremost a newly disabled person is in a new world and in a new moment in life. Not only do they have to deal with becoming disabled but now they must learn about their sexuality all over again. What I mean is, they must find out what works for them. What gives them that feeling of release of intimacy and of fulfillment? I was lucky enough to have been doing my rehabilitation with a guy who was a quadriplegic for over twenty-five years. He had broken his leg and was back for therapy to help with his transfers and strengthening. We roomed together, and I was able to talk privately with him about how sex was as a disabled person.

He told me things I really had a hard time believing as I could not comprehend how it was possible. He told me that everyone orgasms; some do it several times a day. I was like several times a day? He laughed and said yes but it's not what you're thinking. He said the next time you sneeze take a moment and think about your senses and what and how you felt. He proceeded to say that a sneeze is an orgasm (in a sense).

Think about when you are getting ready to sneeze. There is a build-up of anticipation, and then there is even the "almost sneeze" that can be followed by the "big sneeze." Feel the sensation that goes through your body, the small shiver you feel after it is done, and then the euphoric feeling of release after it is over. The breathlessness you feel as your body settles down. That my friend is an orgasm, whether it's been proven or not. I guess what he was saying was there are other feelings you can experience that are very close to the actual release of ejaculation or the sensation of experiencing it.

For most quadriplegics they have limited sensation from the top of the chest down. The level at which paralysis starts can be very sensitive for most. I discovered that my ears are incredibly sensitive to the point that I really can't stand when someone touches them. But I also found one time (when me and my wife were making love) that she was breathing heavily around my ear. The heat of her breath and the touch of her lips combined with the start of her orgasm gave me an incredible sensation.

My body started to have that feeling of shivers going up my spine and just total release as she nibbled on my ear. He said my body slightly convulsed for what seemed like a full minute and afterward it was like total release. Me and my wife just laid there together in sexual bliss as she had given me an orgasm, and I had given her one as well.

My roommate in the rehabilitation center asked me where I was paralyzed, and I told him that my paralysis is just below my nipple area on my chest. To this end, I noticed a sensitivity to my nipples whenever they were touched. To this day I can never tell him how much I appreciated our talks as it opened a whole new world for me and my sexuality with my wife.

Now that's not to say that everything is perfect, and sex is just like it was before I was injured, but the sensation of making love and sharing that time with my wife and being able to satisfy each other and be intimate is unbelievable.

Anyway, you will find below a bunch of questions I've been asked regarding sex (and other people in chairs have been asked). I hope you find the answers informative.

31. Can you still have sex?

I think I answered it in the previous paragraph, but yes, most people in wheelchairs can have sex!

32. Can you orgasm?

Again, I think I answered this already but yes, orgasms can be achieved. It takes a partner willing to be experimental and accepting of how to sexually please their partner. Remember, part of the orgasm is in our brains and how we want to be pleased. I think the sensation of feeling the heat of another against your skin is almost orgasmic as it is.

33. How is sex different?

Another difference (other than what was explained earlier) is I feel I'm a better lover! And no, I'm not bragging. But I feel when I was able-bodied, I didn't spend enough time with my lover. It was trying to please them while I was being pleased and hope everything worked out. Most of the time when I would ejaculate that was it and even the cuddling afterward became an afterthought. I can honestly say that I take a whole lot more time with my wife now and try to satisfy her in every way I can. Yes, you could say she is spoiled but she's worth it. Because I'm not in a hurry to be pleased I'm able to take time with her and the touching and caressing is so much more enjoyable now that I'm not out for myself for satisfaction.

34. Do you still desire sex?

Yes, Yes, Yes! I think for some reason I desire it more than before! It's a little hard to explain but I'll try my best. You see when I'm out of my chair I feel I'm free from my wheelchair. And when I'm in bed with my wife I feel like a man. Vickie and I have been married now for over twenty-six years, and I feel we are very good sexually together. She knows how to please me and takes the time to help me get into the position we want and does it with love and compassion in her eyes.

35. Can you still get an erection?

Being paralyzed usually means everything below the place in the spinal cord has been affected. For the very few (but very lucky) that can get an erection and sustain it for penetration…life is good. For others if you can achieve an erection, they usually are not full and normally don't last for sexual intercourse. Thanks to modern medicine we now have a pill that will help get *and keep* an erection for intercourse. For some though it will not work. There are other ways though that one can still employ in order to get *and maintain* an erection.

There is a manual pump that pulls blood into the penis to get it hard. A thick rubber circular band is then pulled over the penis constricting the base of it and not allowing blood to flow back out. For those that use this device they had better hope that they don't have any sensation, or this might be very painful.

The other technique is even worse! Medicine is

injected into the base of the penis and the medicine causes the blood vessels to fill causing an erection. As with the pills, if an erection lasts over four hours, they must go to the emergency room to have them manually help relieve the erection, by cold temperature or through the use of saline solutions.

36. Can you ejaculate?

Most quadriplegics and paraplegics cannot ejaculate outside of the penis. I say outside because an ejaculation can happen retrograde in which the ejaculatory goes back into the bladder rather than coming out the penis. For other disabilities, ejaculation is a possibility and condoms should be used to prevent pregnancy. Yes, you can still get pregnant as a quadriplegic woman, and a male can still ejaculate enough to get a woman pregnant. Condoms should still be worn even if you don't ejaculate because pre-semen can still come out and get into the vagina to cause a pregnancy.

37. Can you still be spontaneous?

Yes and no. Yes, spontaneity can still be achieved. The question is, is it the same as able-bodied spontaneity? The answer is probably no. If you and your woman are heavily kissing and she is wanting to sexually please you and you cannot achieve an erection, she can still orally stimulate you even though you do not have an erection.

Remember in the previous paragraphs that I said the area just below the paralysis is very sensitive and can cause orgasmic feelings if stimulated. One way is (while orally stimulating your partner) to reach up with your hands and stimulate the section of their body closest to their paralysis.

The nipple areas are usually pretty sensitive for most and the sensation of feeling your partner orally stimulate you while stimulating the sensitive area on your body can be great. And just when you think you can't take the stimulation anymore, if they lightly bite you, it can set off fireworks within your brain enough to cause light convulsions. That is something I highly recommend you explore, because it is unbelievable!

38. Were you afraid to make love the first time after you were paralyzed?

Oh, so much! There were so many things that go through one's mind: *are they going to be sexually satisfied? are you going to be able to achieve the erection? will it stay hard? will I get too excited and have an accident? can I make it feel normal to her?* All these things go through your mind, but if you talk about it and explain what needs to be done then there is a very good chance it will be enjoyable for both parties.

39. Do you still feel sexy or wanted?

As we all get older, we feel we are not as sexy or as desirable as we did when we were younger. It's still the same for the disabled. Yet as a paraplegic or quadriplegic or anyone that has lost their stomach muscles will know, you can get the dreaded bloated stomach (I call it the para pouch). This is the stomach that makes a woman look pregnant even though she isn't. It can also make a man look pregnant as well! ☺

The legs atrophy and the muscles disappear making the legs look like skin wrapped around a bone. These are things we find physically unappealing as a disabled person, and we can't see how someone can find us attractive. My wife says she thinks I'm sexy and she wants me all the time. But I can't see what she sees in me. I guess it's the same for her where she thinks she has put on some weight and how could I find her sexy, but as God as my witness, I love every curve she has and find her irresistible and can't wait until we are all alone and it's only me she wants to be with!

40. Can you still get into different positions?

Different positions are still attainable with pillows or a wedge. One thing that one should take into consideration is that if you are using the pill or injection with the woman being on top, the blood might be able to flow back out of the penis causing the penis to go soft. That is one advantage to using the pump: the blood is trapped in the penis and the penis stays harder, which can allow for more positions.

The drawback to the pump is the penis gets cold as the blood flow is not circulating. For the pill, the missionary position allows for the blood to flow down to the penis allowing for blood flow thus a warmer and harder penis.

With a wedge you can enter from behind as the woman's butt is elevated. Sideways is a problematic position as penetration is difficult and with limited to no abdominal muscles thrusting might not be able to be achieved. There is also a machine out called the "Intimate Rider" which will allow individuals to get into different positions. Sex is still very enjoyable as it allows one to feel less disabled when making love!

On the Lighter Side 4

While I was still in rehabilitation, we had a patio that had a grill on it that was able to be used by people that were doing their rehabilitation. Well, a buddy of mine was going to cook hamburgers and hotdogs for a few of us. He was a paraplegic like me but said he was very good at cooking on the grill. Well the type of grill they had allowed the wheelchair to get up under it with your legs so you could reach inside the grill.

My buddy was a very tall guy and his knees sat high in his wheelchair. While cooking he got too close to the grill with his knees and after a while we smelt something like burning bacon, that's when my buddy looked down and his leg was up against the grill and the bacon smell we smelt was in fact my buddy's leg being burnt by the grill.

He could not feel his legs because he was paralyzed, and he got a pretty severe burn on his knee. We all said we would pass on the grilled knee! He just laughed and said thank God I can't feel it! We all busted out laughing, but we knew it was serious and that he needed to seek out professional medical attention.

Chapter 5

41. Do you still play sports?

Yes, I am very active in sports. The competitive nature is still in me, and it helps me stay in shape which (in turn) helps with my transfers. I still enjoy bowling and hand-cycling, and I have tried other sports. But I still love bowling the best. I was never any good at basketball and feel I'm even worse trying to play it in the wheelchair. Same with tennis. I was never any good at it. However, I could hit the most home runs. Unfortunately, "home runs" only count in baseball and not tennis. I think sports are a great way to get your mind off your disability. If you have competitive juices in your body, it just takes *participating in sports* (you don't have to be great at it) to find something in which you excel. For me as an ex-professional bowler, bowling is in my blood. So, I try to compete as much as possible. I have won tournaments from my wheelchair, and the feeling of conquering my opponents is still thrilling to me.

In the winter of 2016, I was asked to try out to be a bobsled driver on the Olympic bobsled track located in Park City, Utah. I was very hesitant and unsure of what I was about to attempt. I had just turned fifty years old and really felt out of my element! I listened very closely to other athletes and tried to absorb as much information as I could. And when we had our first competition I not only didn't wreck, but I won the first event! I competed on the team for two more years; even competed in the World Cup Championships! I retired from bobsledding in 2017 after we got word that it might be a Paralympic sport in future Paralympic events. I felt I would be too old to compete and decided to leave it to the younger bobsledders!

42. When did you start bowling again?

I started bowling again about four weeks after returning home and adjusting to my new life in a wheelchair. I was told while I was in the hospital that I would never be able to bowl with my right arm again due to all the damage that had been done to it. I'm not sure if it was all the games of practice and how strong my right arm was before the car accident l, but I'd regained enough strength in my right arm to be able to push a manual wheelchair. So, I decided to try bowling again. To my surprise I was able to bowl with my right arm still, and it didn't hurt that bad. The first tournament I bowled in I came in first, because I was bowling so much higher than my usual average.

43. What tournaments have you won since being in the wheelchair?

My first tournament was the Virginia/North Carolina Championships. Then I won the Eastern Regional Wheelchair Championship and won them again four years later. Just recently I was part of a team that won the Utah City Tournament. I will be bowling in the Las Vegas Invitational in December of 2019 and plan to bowl in the 2020 National Wheelchair Championships.

44. Did you ever win a professional bowler's tournament?

Unfortunately, no I've never won a professional tournament as a bowler while on the tour. I would like to point out though that I had cashed-in the last three out of four tournaments Additionally, I've bowled-in and made the top twenty-four finals once and came in twelfth as my highest finishing position in a regional professional tournament.

As I look back on my time on the tour, I can honestly say that I was a decent bowler, but there are guys out on the tour that have more natural ability in their pinky finger than I possessed in my whole body. The key to my game was consistency. I could get locked-in on a lane, and I could hang with the best of them, but my game had very little adjustability in it, and I could lose my concentration and delivery quickly leaving me scratching my head as everyone around me shot some big numbers.

45. Do you use different chairs for sports?

Wheelchair sports chairs should fit a lot tighter than everyday chairs, because you want the chair to be an extension of your body. Whenever you move, the chair should move with you. Racing wheelchairs should fit tight as well, as you want all the inertia of your push to be transferred to the push rims creating more speed. You usually want your sports chair to be much lighter than your everyday chair so it will be more responsive. But for me with a bowling wheelchair you want the heavier the better, as you do not want the chair to move while you swing the ball back and forth. So, because weight is a good strategy, I bowl from a power wheelchair to get as little chair movement while I'm delivering the ball.

46. How many wheelchairs do you have?

Right now, only five ☺. My wife keeps telling me if I bring home another wheelchair, it can stay but I must go! So, I think I'm going to keep it at five for right now. Now some may ask, "Why would anyone need five wheelchairs?" If you think of a pair of shoes, most people have two or three, and if they are active and play sports and camp and fish, then more than likely they have *several pairs of shoes*. Well, it's no different regarding wheelchairs.

I have my everyday chair; the one I use most all the time. It's the chair that gets beat up and scratched and just takes the brunt of everyday use and abuse. You usually want something lightweight that you can easily take apart to put in your car or a friend's car. By using it each day, you tend to break parts which require repair, thus needing the use of a backup wheelchair.

The backup wheelchair needs to be almost as good as the primary chair as it might have to be used for a long period of time due to lengthy repair times for chairs. Then I have my "bling-bling" chair (as I call it). It's the chair I do my speaking and presentations in.

The "bling-bling" chair is kept shiny and clean and has spinners on the wheels that are shaped like dollar signs and the actual spinners are shaped like cents. The back upholstery has flames on it; the front wheels and the casters all light up when I roll around. The whole chair is highly polished aluminum which shines like no tomorrow!

Then there's my bowling power wheelchair. It's used *just for bowling*. This chair must stay inside just about all the time other than taking it to the bowling alley. This is to ensure that there is nothing on the wheels or casters that might get on the lanes while bowling. The lanes are used by other people that must wear special bowling shoes, so I must make sure I'm not getting anything on the lanes.

The biggest headache happens when it snows or rains! It's such a pain making sure the chair is completely dried off and that not even a drop gets on the lane. Believe it or not, that one drop getting on the approaches where the bowlers throw the ball can make a person stick or not be able to slide when throwing the ball, which can really mess them up. And if a person steps wrong, they might even get hurt from stumbling when throwing the ball. But the absolute worst is when it snows!

During snowy conditions, I decide to either

arrive an hour early or to not even go—it's that bad. Think about it, rolling around in the snow getting snow and ice in the tread of the tires and up in the wheel wells and the splattering of water and ice underneath the chair. It would be almost impossible to ensure that the chair was totally dry. Thus, this is the main reason why I sit out sometimes.

47. Do you bowl in a wheelchair bowling league?

Unfortunately, no I do not bowl on a wheelchair bowling league. I had a wheelchair bowling league back in Virginia Beach that I bowled with, but right now I am the only one in the league that is in a wheelchair. But I don't mind, I rather enjoy beating the able-bodied at bowling!

The good thing about bowling in a wheelchair league is that you can learn from others whereas in the able-bodied leagues everyone tries to help you. But they are not in a wheelchair so it's hard to listen to someone that's not in your shoes (so to speak). People have asked me why I don't start one here in Utah, and my answer is kind of selfish: it's because I went through a lot of difficult times getting the league in Virginia Beach going and frankly, I don't want to go through those headaches again. Not that I'm saying it'll never happen, but I'm just not interested right now.

Additionally, I'm very competitive, and I know if I got a wheelchair league going, I'd want to get a wheelchair bowling tournament going and that's where I'd see problems forming. I don't want to organize another tournament, because it was a nightmare. Thank God I had Ray and Anna Korchak in Virginia Beach, because they basically ran the whole tournament. I just helped get it started and off the ground.

48. Do you travel to sports tournaments?

Just about all the tournaments I bowl in are out of town, which requires a lot of traveling. Most people don't realize the extensive preparation and headaches someone in a wheelchair goes through to travel to a tournament. For most it's just packing, making the reservations, and then making the journey. This is not the case for someone in a wheelchair. Even making the reservations can start the whole trip off on the wrong foot.

When making a reservation you must check on the availability of a wheelchair-accessible room. Now one might say you just ask for a wheelchair-accessible room, right? Unfortunately, not. You see there are so many variables when getting a room, you really need to ask the right questions. If you call and ask for a handicap room, you might get one with just a grab bar on the wall in the bathroom. If you ask for a wheelchair- accessible room, they must make sure your wheelchair can get into the room and the bathroom.

I try to get online and check out the rooms. Most of the time they don't have the accessible rooms pictured, so you are at the mercy of accepting the word of the person on the phone to give you the right information. I always call the day before and make sure they have a wheelchair accessible room available, and I always guarantee that the room will be held until I get there. There is nothing worse than making a reservation just to get there and have your room given away. So, my advice is to do your homework and make sure everything is good before you set out on your adventure.

49. How is it to fly with your wheelchair?

Let's talk about being nervous when flying with a manual or power wheelchair. I have heard horror stories from other wheelchair users when flying. I have witnessed how they load and unload wheelchairs from the airplane, and it is scary! But let me back up first because you need to know a few things before you even make the reservations.

The first thing to know is what type of batteries you have in your chair. You must have gel cell batteries that are non-spillable. I say, "gel cell," because these are the words you must say to make sure that you even get on the plane. You see, the gate attendant is going to ask you if they are gel batteries cause they want to make sure they won't possibly spill acid while in the plane's cargo hold. Now I know there are sealed lead acid batteries that are non-spillable, but if you want to try to get on the plane with a reservationist that doesn't understand that then you will be taking a big risk.

Gel cell non-spillables are the best to fly with as

there should be no question about them being approved.

A second thing I do is I take the joystick off my chair and carry it with me on the plane. This can be problematic if the wires are all wire-tied to the chair. Therefore, I would go through a checklist before you go to make sure you remember to take the joystick. Now why (you might ask) do I take off my joystick off when flying? Well, you must disengage your power wheelchair so they can roll it to the conveyer belt to put luggage on the plane. Once they get it there, they cannot put it on the belt because it will roll off. Most of the luggage handlers don't know how to engage and disengage the chairs so they lay the power wheelchair on its side to get it up the belt. Then once it is at the top of the belt, they don't put it on its wheels. No, they then drag the chair on its side into the cargo hold.

Can you imagine your joystick being dragged across the belly of the plane since its laying on its side? That's why I take mine off, to prevent damage to a $1,500.00 (or even more expensive) joystick. Manual wheelchairs are much easier to fly with as you don't have nearly as many concerns.

Another tip I can give someone in a wheelchair who wants to fly is try to always gate check your chair even if your next flight is going out of the next gate. The reason I do this is I've learned that you never know when there will be a flight problem or cancelation. You don't want your chair to lie on the bottom of a plane somewhere while you are stuck in one of the airport chairs with the fluttering wheel. Also, and in the worst circumstance, the flight is canceled. Then you must stay overnight in one of their airport chairs, and it's not a pretty picture.

One final tip is this: always take your pouch and cushion off your chair and take them on the plane with you even if you're not going to sit on your cushion on the plane. This is so you'll at least have it with you in case the worst-case scenario occurs.

50. Has the airlines ever lost your chair?

No, and thank God, knock on wood, cross fingers, say "Hail Mary," or whatever I need to do to make it never happen as well! That's why gate checking your chair is so important. You know the chair is getting off the plane when you do.

A lot of the problems people experience occur during the reservation process, i.e., they don't leave enough time between flights. So, they think something like, "I'll just get into an airport chair and then head to my next flight." That's when nature calls, and they must go to the bathroom. As a result, they miss their next flight and their chair goes to the next stop without them. Possibilities of a lost chair go up quite a bit when that happens!

On the Lighter Side 5!

Whenever I'm alone things just happen! I was leaving my parent's home and pressed the button for the garage door to close and then I propelled myself as fast as I could to make it out of the garage before the door shut on me.

I made it just in time before the door shut. I'd pulled the car up to the garage door as close as I could to allow others to park in the driveway as well. Well everyone had left already, and I was all alone, but I had made it out of the garage and was going around the car to get in. I opened the door and made my transfer into the car. While transferring, my brake came loose, and my chair proceeded to turn away from me.

With one brake turned on, the chair circled around and somehow ended up behind the car. So, picture it: I'm now there sitting in the car while my chair is now positioned behind the car. Additionally, my car was right up against the garage door, so there was no way to move up and no way to move back.

I thought of just backing up and pushing the chair out of the way, but the chair wouldn't budge. So, all I could do was lay on the horn and hope to be saved by a neighbor who finally arrived to rescue me. ☺

Chapter 6

51. Have you ever fallen out of your wheelchair?

Yes, I have but not that often. I generally have excellent balance so I can usually catch myself when I lose my balance and feel myself falling. For someone that's in a wheelchair, believe me, this is a huge fear. Being paralyzed, or not having feeling in your lower extremities, can be very scary when you fall. Not having sensation or being able to tell when you have really hurt yourself is a big problem for those individuals. If they do not know that they have badly sprained an ankle or even broke a bone can cause severe swelling and open the possibility of getting a blood clot. Blood clots can be fatal if they travel into the blood vessels and go into the heart. So, falls from a wheelchair can be serious.

One of the most memorable falls I had occurred while me and my wife were dancing, and I had placed my jacket on the push handle of my wheelchair. The push handle is on the back of the wheelchair, and I forgot this because I was distracted. We started dancing around, and I was doing wheelies moving to the beat when my jacket got caught under my wheel causing my wheelchair to get stuck in the wheelie position.

What happened next felt like slow-motion video. I felt the chair start tipping back and with no way to stop it, I flipped over. Whenever you go over backwards in a wheelchair you can count on hitting your head on the ground and sometimes very hard. It about knocked me out, and I had a terrible headache the rest of the night.

52. Have you ever fallen in the shower?

Falls in the shower or bathroom are very common. As a matter of fact, if there is going to be a place where you must be careful it's in the bathroom. People with limited mobility and poor balance have the most falls while in the shower. Shower chairs help someone with limited mobility. However, whenever you add in the element of water you are also introducing a whole new dynamic.

Our skin becomes slippery and surfaces become frictionless. One false move will send even the heaviest person into a speeding downfall onto the shower floor. Now I don't know if you've ever had to pick someone up that is naked and soaking wet and not able to help, but it is very dangerous. This is true not only for the person who has fallen but for the person helping (as they are now vulnerable too). I fell one time in the shower and had no one home to help me get back into the chair. It was quite nerve-wracking as I had to systematically work through the steps I needed to do to get myself back into either the shower chair or my wheelchair.

The first thing I needed to do was get my cushion off my wheelchair so that I'm not sitting on the hard surface of the shower floor. I then had to dry myself off, and dry the shower chair the best that I could in order to make it less slippery. Then and while using the seat of the shower chair as a surface, I used my left hand to push my body up and used my right hand (held in a fist) to manipulate the corner of the cushion. Then I raised my butt up just high enough to get a butt cheek onto the seat. Still with most of my body not on the seat of the chair, I pushed with my right hand (still held in a fist) inching my body up onto the seat of the shower chair. For me it was a successful transfer, for others that do not have the strength to make a transfer like that, it would have been hell. I know they'd be frightened to death, because you cannot stay prone on the floor for long. Sitting on a hard surface even though you have your cushion underneath you can still cause pressure sores as you do not have the ability to relieve the pressure from you sitting on bony prominences.

53. Do you do dishes?

Yes, believe it or not I do dishes! It is difficult getting your wheelchair close enough to the sink to do the dishes, but if you angle your chair to the cabinets you can reach in to get to the dishes that have been placed into the sink. There are special modifications that can be done to make the cabinets more wheelchair friendly so the front of the wheelchair can get under the sink. But with the proper angle you can get close enough to do them. So, ladies if your man says he can't get close enough he might be lying!

54. Do you vacuum?

I have been seen vacuuming at one time or another but to tell you the honest truth, no. I usually don't do the vacuuming in my home. Not that I can't but the wire and the hose and just being able to move it around is cumbersome, so my wife or my daughter usually take on this household chore.

55. Do you do the wash?

One mistake when we had our home built? We did not allow enough room in the washroom for the baskets of clothes, the washer and the dryer, and my wheelchair. In a pinch I'll do the wash if I must, but that is another chore my daughter or my wife tend to handle for me.

56. Do you clean the bathroom?

Yes, I do! The bathroom is my chore, and I've told my wife I don't mind doing it as it is usually me that has it looking like a mess. Not that I like doing it…if I said that I'd be lying. However, I feel Vickie should not have to clean up my mess.

57. Do you do windows?

This was a funny question, but no. I don't do our windows. Never thought of it. But I think it might be another accessibility problem. To clarify, I don't think it's impossible, because I always feel if there's a will, then there's a way.

58. Do you do the lawn?

No, I don't do our lawn. And again, it's not that I can't, but my wife does it because she enjoys doing the yard.

59. Do you do the garden?

I never had a green thumb, but I have friends that are in chairs that really have some nice gardens. They planted the rows wide enough to get their chairs in between the plants to do their upkeep and gardening. My wife really enjoys gardening as it gives her time away from everyone, and she can just take care of the plants and take her mind off everything else.

60. Do you work on your own car?

I used to be able to work on my vehicles before I was paralyzed. But we are talking about twenty-four years ago and the cars nowadays look like spaghetti underneath the hoods. So, no, I don't work on my own car. I take it to the Jiffy Lube or local repair shop and have them do the repairs.

On the Lighter Side 6

One of my best friends (who was a double amputee) played in tennis tournaments all the time and was pretty good at them. Well one tournament he went to, they had a banquet at the end of the tournament and they always give away door prizes to all the players. They had great prizes and the organizers got many big companies to donate some merchandise.

Well my friend gets his number drawn to come up and pick up his prize, and as he is heading up there in his chair, he was shaking his head all the way up to the table. When he got there to get his prize, he was handed a very nice pair of socks! Now being a double below-the-knee amputee, you can only imagine the look on his face when he got his prize. However, instead of being disappointed or being unhappy, without any hesitation he puts them on his hands and says, "Thank God they're made of wool or my hands would get cold!"

He was a very classy guy!

Chapter 7

61. What is a pressure sore and how do they happen?

One of the biggest fears of someone in a wheelchair is the dreaded pressure sore. The pressure sore is usually caused when a bony prominence is pressed up against the skin not allowing proper blood flow to the area. This in turn causes a sore to form.

The bad thing about these sores are that they form from the inside, and by the time they are visible at the surface they're already terrible sores. A pressure sore can go all the way to the bone. If it's on the buttocks area they can be as deep as four to five inches.

When a sore is that deep it usually requires hospital care and can take anywhere from six months to even a year to heal up. A skin flap is occasionally done to help close the wound by taking skin from the hip area and sewing up the open sore. The wound must heal from the inside out and once it is closed the body has a better time healing itself if no further pressure is placed on the area. This usually means more time in bed.

That (in itself) can be a problem. You see, the body needs to be turned so no other sores form. This is usually done with a special air mattress that alternates pressure between cells that inflate and deflate. These artificial waves prevent the build-up of pressure on the body.

I know the concept of pressure might be hard to understand, so let me try to explain it. When you sit in a chair you adjust yourself when you get uncomfortable. It may just be a simple shift of your buttocks on a chair, but you in fact change the pressure of your tuberosities.

What are tuberosities? They are the bones which go into the hip sockets—basically they're your butt bones. The coccyx bone is the bone in the center of your butt that also can have a lot of pressure placed on it. These bones are being sat on while someone is sitting in a wheelchair, and if they're not relieved of pressure, they can form a sore. Therefore, they have air and gel cushions to help displace some of the pressure while seated. It's that pressure which causes you to experience the discomfort which stimulates you to shift your weight in the first place.

62. Have you ever broken a bone?

No, and thank God I haven't that I know of. And I say, "I know of," because I had some black and blue skin in the past and had toes that have been swollen for a week at a time. However, eventually the swelling and bruising cleared up. Could it have been a hairline fracture? Very possibly. But I'm so glad I couldn't feel it at that moment!

63. What is a U.T.I.?

A U.T.I. is an abbreviation that stands for "urinary tract infection." It is mostly caused by intermittent catheterization. Catheterization (as I discussed earlier) is where a tube is placed into the urethra to aid in elimination of urine. If done in a non-sterile area the possibility of contracting a urinary infection is high. Urinary infections can be quite serious and on rare occasions, fatal, if not caught soon enough.

64. Why does your leg shake?

A muscle spasm is an involuntary muscle movement causing the muscle to contract. This creates a shaking motion. It is an uncontrolled movement caused by stimulation or a pain indicator or even a signal passed by nerves. Sometimes, it's a sign of toxic pressure.

If they get bad enough, muscle spasms can be controlled by drugs. There is even a medicine pump called a baclofen pump which intermittently injects medicine into one's system to prevent the muscles from contracting.

My spasms are set off by simply hitting a crack in the sidewalk or any unplanned bump to my legs. Thankfully mine are not painful. Therefore, I don't need a baclofen pump, but I do take an oral medicine to keep them at a minimum.

65. How come you can't cough?

I can still cough but just don't have the lung capacity that I once had due to where my paralysis is. I'm paralyzed from the mid-chest area down, which is basically half of my lungs. I can take in a full breath of air. But to cough, I find that I can't take in enough air to get a good cough out. When I get a chest cold, it's very dangerous as I must drop my chest into my lap to force enough air to cough up anything getting into my lungs. For most quadriplegics or individuals who have had their lungs affected, pneumonia is a constant threat. They can get pneumonia due to their inability to excrete phlegm which then collects in the lungs.

66. Have you been in the hospital since your accident?

Luckily, I've only had short stays in the hospital since my accident. There are so many reasons why someone in a wheelchair can end up back in the hospital. Pneumonia, pressure sores, urinary tract infections…these are just a few of the things a disabled person must be careful of while living their life. Smoking, drinking, not timing pressure reliefs, not drinking enough water, drinking too many soft drinks, not eating enough or eating the wrong types of food…these can all put you in the hospital. It is a constant fight just to stay alive.

67. How can you tolerate hospital food?

Now this was a funny question! Tolerate is about the extent of it. I can honestly say that the food in hospitals has actually gotten better over the years. When I was first in the hospital in 1990 the food was terrible. I couldn't wait until I could have non-institutionalized food! I'd lost so much weight and with the food they prepared for me in the hospital, gaining weight was a real challenge. At one point, I only weighed 85 pounds.

When we finally got to Woodrow Wilson Rehab in Fishersville Virginia, I felt I was in heaven. The cooks there were awesome! And it wasn't like you had to have the same thing as everyone else. It was more like a cafeteria setting, and we actually had a menu to order from, but the food was like home-cooked meals.

My favorite was the chicken and rice soup they made; I would order two to three bowls of it. And the desserts were to die for! I'm talking black forest chocolate cake, homemade carrot cake, homemade sundaes, and red velvet wedding cake…unbelievable to say the least. I quickly started to put weight back on and can honestly say I enjoyed it immensely. I guess they figured that most people lose weight while in the hospital and they needed to help with the weight recovery. But there's still nothing better than eating food cooked at home.

68. Do you get sicker now?

Luckily, I've been pretty healthy. Besides the occasional U.T.I. or pressure sore I really don't get that sick. I contribute it to me washing my hands ten to twelve times a day, not that I'm obsessive. No, the reason is because I need to cath four to five times a day and I wash my hands before and after each time I cath.

My immune system has been excellent too. Even if I get a cold, I recover really quick. As a preventative measure, I try to make sure that if someone is sick around me, to try and avoid them.

One problem I know I have is my limited ability to cough. It's always on the forefront of my mind. Thus, I'm careful to try and not to let any sickness get into my lungs. Any place there are sick people…for example, nursing homes…I feel I'm at risk. One of the most common causes of death in a person who is in a wheelchair is pneumonia. With us sitting most of the time and not getting much exercise, the phlegm just increases in the lungs. Add to this an inability to cough fully, and you have a perfect breeding ground for pneumonia to form.

69. Why do you hold your legs?

Most people think I hold my legs because they hurt. I have no feeling in them, so the real reason is two-fold.

The first is this: since my accident my internal

body thermostat does not work the same as it did. My hands are constantly cold, and I put them under my leg to try to keep them warm.

The second reason is because of my leg spasms. I've lost my balance while sitting in the chair many times due to a leg spasm. When my leg starts to spasm, I can stop it by lifting my leg and the spasm will go away. For others who don't have this option, they aren't so lucky. In those situations, the spasm doesn't stop until the muscle gets tired. When a spasm does start because my hand is under my leg I can hold on and not lose my balance and make my spasm go away.

70. Do you have pain now?

I do have a little pain, but I've learned to live with the pain, and it doesn't bother me as much as it did before. Others are not so lucky. Some live with chronic pain and are popping pills constantly just looking for a little relief. The weirdest pain is what they call phantom pain. That's the pain most amputees suffer as they feel they have pain in their leg or arm that has been removed. It can be excruciating pain but there is no way to help alleviate the pain they feel. Yes, it's psychological, but it's all too real for a disabled individual.

On the Lighter Side 7

A friend who was a quadriplegic was independent and always took his dog for a walk. Now, he used a manual wheelchair and pushed his chair with his wrists and the palms of his hands (he could not grip his hand rims because he had no finger dexterity).

Well he attached the leash of the dog to the front of the frame of his wheelchair. The problem was, his dog was a big pit bull, and although it was a very well-trained dog, it had a problem with cats! Well, while he was out for a walk with his dog, a cat jumped out in front of him and the chase was on!

Luckily, because he was a quad he seat-belted himself in the chair and was kind of prepared when his dog took off after the cat. He said his dog chased this cat through yards, mud puddles, a field, through a garage, and landed upside down finally coming to a rest on his neighbor's lawn! The dog comes over to him while he is laying on the ground and starts licking his face as if to say what are you doing you made me miss getting that cat! ☺

Chapter 8

71. How much did your most expensive wheelchair cost?

My insurance bought most of my wheelchairs; my most expensive manual wheelchair cost around $5000.00 (it was made of titanium). My power wheelchair I used for camping was valued at around $8000.00. However, these are not really that expensive compared to the power wheelchairs they have now. Some of the power wheelchairs are running $50,000 to $60,000 dollars or even more.

72. What do you do in case of a flat tire?

The dreaded flat tire can put a damper on any day! Just like with a bicycle if you get a flat tire you cannot roll around, because you'll ruin the rim. I usually run flat free inserts in my wheels. Flat free inserts are solid (and harder) foam tubes that go inside the tire which prevents any punctures (there is no air in them).

Another option is slime tubes. These have a slime substance in them and when there is a puncture the slime oozes into the hole and clogs the puncture. This is very messy when the slime gets in-between the tube and rim, and for that reason I don't like using them. Now when I'm in one of my chairs that doesn't have them, I'm kinda paranoid whenever I see glass or thorns. I don't want to experience a flat tire.

I always have a spare tube in my truck as well as tools to change it out if I should get a flat. Now you might ask, "How do you put air in it? Do you carry around a tire pump too?" My answer would be no. I use these little compressed carbon dioxide air cans that put air into the tube quickly. They're good little gadgets, but you can mess up the amount of air that goes in if you don't have the nozzle on correct. The replacement canisters are a little expensive, but they work well.

73. Why don't you use a power wheelchair instead of a manual wheelchair?

For most people who get a wheelchair through their insurance, they either buy a manual or a power wheelchair according to their disability. If a person can push a manual wheelchair in their home and get into the bathroom and kitchen, then the insurance (more than likely) may deny any powered wheelchair or scooter. For a lot of people that can push around their house, it is sad that they can't get a power wheelchair. They may be able to push around their home, however, once they get outside, they can't make it to the end of the block without having to stop and take a break because they're too tired or weak to push anymore. This really limits an individual regarding their quality of life, because they get stuck at home a lot.

Unfortunately, the insurances really don't care if you ever go outside the home. They only need to provide mobility within the home. If you are in this situation where you can only get a manual wheelchair through your insurance and want to have a power wheelchair to do more things outside of the home, look at your local community and see if they have a refurbishing center or independent living center. Either of these places might have a power wheelchair you could borrow or even purchase from them that is used. Additionally, it will only run a fraction of the price of a new one.

Here in Utah, we have an organization called U.A.T.P. Salt Lake in which wheelchairs are donated to them because a loved one has passed away or someone has grown out of it. Or it could even be that they regained the ability to walk. Nevertheless, they receive in some beautiful chairs. A lot of the time, the little nubs are still on the tires. This means the chair is brand new, and the person it was intended for never really got to use it. Who knows why? It could be as simple as they got sick and just couldn't get well enough to use it.

When UATP Salt Lake gets in a wheelchair, they refurbish it to its original manufacturer's specifications, they clean and sterilize it, and they make sure the chair is in good working order. Only when all these conditions are met do they sell it back to the community. However, they only charge the amount it took to get it refurbished. I've seen power chairs go out the door for around $400.00 to $500.00, and that's with new batteries in them! It's a great organization, and you should really check

and see if there's one in your community. If there
isn't, then start one!

74. What is the longest wheelie you have done?

In rehabilitation they taught us how to do
wheelies and go over uneven terrain. For me I
learned how to do wheelies very well and can do
one for a really long distance. Heck, I get up into a
wheelie and can dance in a wheelie for quite a
while! One person bet me once that I couldn't do a
wheelie from one end of a football field to the other
(and do so while on grass). Well I'm proud to say
that's one bet I won!

So, I guess about a hundred yards would have to
be the answer to this question.

Now if we're talking a continuous wheelie with
just one push and glide until the end, then I have an
answer for that too. I'd say it would have to be
around a few hundred yards going downhill. For
this one, I put the chair up into a wheelie and then
let gravity take over. The only problem was that
even with gloves on, the hand rims got hot to the
touch trying to regulate my speed, and I almost
burned myself!

75. Can you go down steps in your chair?

In case of a fire and the elevators were out of
working condition, we learned how to go down

steps. In case you don't know this, it's very difficult going down, and it's even more difficult going up while sitting in a wheelchair. There are a few techniques they teach you in rehabilitation, but the one that I was able to do the best was the technique where you go down backwards in the wheelchair and (holding onto the handrail) you lower yourself down each step slowly until you get to the bottom. This takes a lot of strength to do and most individuals can't do it.

76. Can you go upstairs?

Going up a flight of stairs is one of the most difficult things anyone in a wheelchair will ever have to do. There's a technique to this as well, but I myself have not been able to do it. The technique takes a lot of upper body strength to hang onto the handrail and to lift your hips to make the chair lighter and swivel your body to pull you up the stairs while in the chair. You must google going upstairs in a wheelchair and see what I mean. It really is amazing to see!

77. Can you jump ramps?

Well I must admit that I'm not that young anymore! In my wild years I might have tried it but now at my age I'm a little more cautious. The reason? Well the aches and pains don't go away as fast. Besides there is a young guy out there doing

ramp jumps in coliseums! If you haven't heard of
Aaron Fatheringham you have to check out this
daredevil, because he will amaze you! Please go
check out his website at
www.aaronfatheringham.com. He is the first to ever
land a front flip in a wheelchair. He has done back
flips, front flips, skate parks, skate ramps…just
about anything done with a skateboard, this man
can do it in a wheelchair.

78. Have you ever gotten into a fight in your wheelchair?

When I was just twenty-six years old and feeling
like I was still the man that could take care of
himself in a fight, I pressed my luck a couple of
times. However, I never got into a fist fight while in
my wheelchair. There was one close call though,
and I'll tell you about it.

I had just started dating my soon-to-be wife,
Vickie, and we'd gone to a restaurant to have dinner
with friends. Well while I was looking out the
window, I saw this guy walk by my car and spit.
Now, at the angle I was sitting at, it looked as if he
had spit right on my car. I was infuriated and took
off towards the door to meet this guy as he walked
in. I can't really tell you why I was so mad at this
guy. Was it because I felt like he was spitting on my
car because I was parked in a handicapped spot?
Was it because I thought that he thought my car
didn't belong there? Or was it just my inner self
lashing out because I'm in a wheelchair for the rest

of my life?

Well, whatever it was I met him at the door and ran into his legs as hard as I could yelling the whole time, "Why the hell did you spit on my car!?"

This poor guy had no idea what this crazy guy in a wheelchair (who just barreled into him as he walked into the door) was talking about. For the life of me I don't know what stopped this guy from beating the crap out of me. Wheelchair or not, he should have decked me. He was mad as hell at me, and he wanted to know what my problem was, and I yelled back, "You spit on my @@#%%$@ car!" He yelled back "I did not! I spit on the ground!"

Well we went out to the parking lot (with my friends and his friends both in tow). We were ready to rumble. Once we got out there, there was (in fact) a spot where he had spit on the ground and not on my car! I was so embarrassed, and Vickie who had backed me the whole way was embarrassed as well.

My friends who were ready to fight, just looked at me and shook their heads, and they said "Yep, he hasn't changed, a bit, He's the same ole Ken!" They all started laughing and I apologized to this poor guy who was going to have two nice bruises on his shins the next morning. As I laid in bed that night going over everything that had happened, I couldn't get over why I snapped like that. I had some soul searching to do and I had to start immediately before it got out of hand.

79. Has your wheel ever fallen off your wheelchair?

Most people who are not around someone that uses a wheelchair are unaware that they have chairs that have an option of having a quick release axle which will allow the wheel to be removed from the chair. This quick release axle helps lessen the weight of the wheelchair, and it helps make it possible to fit into a trunk of a car. So, I was kinda surprised that I was asked this question, but the answer is, yes. It has fallen off while I have been in my wheelchair!

I was going down the sidewalk at the beach with some friends of mine, and the wheel felt like it was wobbling. Before I could realize that the wheel was getting further away from my chair, my chair collapsed onto the ground and my wheel rolled away!

You see, when my friends were putting my chair back together after taking it out of the trunk, they did not pull on the wheel to be sure it was on securely. It was also my fault for not double-checking to be sure it was on tight. On a quick release axle there is a button you push that makes two little ball bearings at the end of the axle retract into the axle which allows the wheel to be taken off. When you put the wheel on the chair you must ensure that the two ball bearings pop back out which lock the wheel onto the chair.

When they put my wheel on, one of the ball bearings had not popped back out which allowed my wheel to come off. Now here I am laying on my side and my fiends start laughing at me as they walked away! I really think I need to get new friends! ☺

80. How do you reach cabinets while in your wheelchair?

Being in the wheelchair has its disadvantages when trying to reach up into cabinets or closets. They make power wheelchairs that can raise up to the height of a standard kitchen cabinet. They even have some that can stand you up to reach into them. They are expensive chairs, and if you can't afford one then you must learn to improvise.

I can reach the bottom of the raised cabinets in my kitchen, but I keep most all my plates and cups and food at a level where I can access it from my wheelchair. I have a center island in my kitchen that has a spinning carousel where I usually store everything that I use. Then when I want something, I spin the carousel around until the item comes around that I need.

Inventors have come out with cabinets that have rails and rollers on them that allow the cabinet to be pulled with a handle located on the bottom of the cabinet. These can lower to the height of the lower cabinets which allow you access into them, then once you're finished using them, they are spring-loaded and return to the position where the cabinets are located. Although they are a little more expensive, they make accessibility look normal in the kitchen.

On the Lighter Side 8

A friend told me this story of a wheelchair basketball team that was flying to get to their tournament a few states away. As usual they board all the wheelchair users first to get them situated in their seats. Well the airlines only had a few onboard chairs that they could use. You see a person's wheelchair is too big to take someone onto an airplane, so they must use a special chair that the airlines have for just this purpose to get you onto the airplane.

Well, they were loading the team onto the plane when one of the double leg amputee players was lifted by another player who could stand up into one of the overhead luggage compartments. After he got in there, he closed the compartment and waited until other passengers were able to board the plane. When a businesswoman went to put her suitcase up into the overhead compartment the double amputee yelled, "Close the door I'm sleeping!"

The whole team busted out with laughter and the lady fell into her seat laughing as well!

Chapter 9

81. Do you go on roller coasters?

I have a love/hate relationship with roller coasters! I love the thrill but can't stand the anticipation of finally getting into the coaster to take my turn. Actually, this goes for any thrilling ride in an amusement park; you can bet I'm up for it with one exception: no shoulder harnesses. Being paralyzed and not having feeling, I can't stand having just a lap bar or belt.

We went on a ride at Busch Gardens in Williamsburg, Virginia, and it was called Apollo's Chariot. It only had a bar that dropped across your lap. I never felt secure that I was not going to come out of the seat! Several times, I felt my butt come up off the seat and was not sure of my safety. Yes, I was very secure in the seat and had no way of coming out of the coaster, but the anxiety just wasn't worth it.

Ever since then I avoided any thrill rides that don't have a harness that comes over my upper body. I know I know I'm a wimp! ☺

And on this topic, there are benefits to being disabled. One benefit is that we could ride two times. Additionally, we got to go to the front of the lines through the exits. Now you might think that's unfair. Just because someone's disabled shouldn't mean they automatically qualify for a privilege that isn't available for able-bodied folk. But many rides are outside and, *in the sun,* which for most disabled people is not a good thing (most disabled people cannot be in the heat for long periods of time). The amusement park knew this, and their thoughtfulness made it possible for me (and other disabled people like me) to enjoy the rides just like everyone else.

82. Are most restaurants accessible?

For the most part just about every restaurant I've been to has been accessible. Thanks to the Americans with Disabilities Act, which was signed into law back in 1990 by President George H. W. Bush, restaurants must be accessible for all if they're open to the public. However, occasionally I'll go someplace that will not have proper access.

Instead of getting all bent out of shape over it, I'll point it out to the owner or manager. Sometimes I may be specific regarding what the barrier might be and give them a possible recommendation of a way to make it more accessible for others. But that's not to say that I won't go back to see if it has been changed. If not, I'll let them know if they don't get it changed that I'll report them and possibly be a pain in their side until it is fixed.

Please know that this is not because I'm a jerk or feel entitled. No, it's because I'm like anyone else when I go out: I want to have fun just like the next person, but I hate being inconvenienced because someone doesn't want to obey the law. It's those people who don't obey the law, who don't realize the pain and frustration they inflict on another human being, who need an attitude correction.

And why would they do this anyway? Maybe they think making their restaurant accessible might cost too much. The truth is, a lot of the time the barrier can be rectified with a simple modification. I know that many disabled people might not choose to say anything because they don't want to bring attention to themselves, or they are too embarrassed to speak up. I am not one of these people, so I'll let them know!

83. Do you know when you are hungry?

Most disabled individuals know when they are hungry but there are others that cannot feel when they are hungry or for that matter when they are full! Memories of hunger and taste are all some other disabled individuals have due to a problem with their senses. Not being able to feel when you're full is really a problem for individuals as they can develop eating disorders and stomach ulcers due to the stomach stretching. I myself can feel when I'm hungry, but I have another complication that limits the amount that I can eat.

84. Do you know when you are full?

I can feel when I'm full but about a couple of years after my accident I started experiencing urinary tract infections or bladder infections. My bladder was very small and whenever I would need to urinate (because I was taking medicine that would prevent me from urinating on accident) I started developing muscles on my bladder that would try to force the urine out. The result was that it would reflex back up into my kidneys.

Well to alleviate this problem they had to go in and take some of my larger intestines and sew it onto my bladder to make it larger (to hold more volume) which in turn would prevent the muscles on my bladder from trying to make me void. But the result of this procedure had unforeseen consequences. You see, the average person has storage in their large intestine for the food they've eaten that's processing. But in my system (which no longer has this storage) I can only eat a certain amount of food in a day or it will cause me to have an accident or uncontrolled bowel movement. It's just another situation that I must deal with in my life!

85. Do you get mad when an able-bodied person parks in a handicapped parking space?

When I do see someone that parks in a space reserved for the disabled and see them jump out of their car and run into the store, it does get me upset. I know there are hidden disabilities and sometimes you may think that a person is just being lazy and using the disabled parking space. However, there is a reason why they designate it for the disabled. My main complaint is when a person parks too close to the lines and does not leave enough room for you to park and get your wheelchair out of the car. And most of the time it's someone else disabled that parks crooked or too close!

When I used to have a van, I would always see people park in the van accessible spots when they didn't have a van even if there were plenty of regular disabled spots available. I just hope people will learn that (even though they have a disabled placard or license plate) you should still be considerate and take a spot that is not van accessible if you are able to do so.

One local problem we have here in Utah is regarding winter snow removal. In Salt Lake City, the snowplows that clean the parking lots will push all the snow into the corner of the parking lot. Sometimes this happens to be the disabled parking spot or the lined loading zones for vans!

Anyway, if you are reading my book, please listen. Even if it's just for a second or a minute, please do not park in a disabled spot if you are not disabled. You never know when you might just become disabled and need one of these spaces!

86. What do you do if there is not a ramp?

Accessibility is a major problem for someone in a wheelchair. If there is not a ramp, it will require that the person in the wheelchair be manually lifted over a curb or up steps which is not only dangerous for the person in the chair but also dangerous for whomever is giving them assistance. The

Americans with Disabilities Act of 1990 has provided access for so many people because of its requirements for businesses and public places. However, there are still places that do not have ramps or clear pathways for a person in a wheelchair to access. Being in a wheelchair for over twenty-nine years I've seen many changes for the better in public access (and changes regarding acceptance of a disability). We've come a long way, but there is still a long way to go.

87. How do you go shopping?

Being independent has its downfalls. Sometimes you want to be able to do things by yourself, but even the simplest things can become such a chore when going shopping. From the time you get into the parking lot of the shopping center you'll be faced with challenges. First will be the parking space and finding one that is available. Once you find a space you then need to get the chair out of the car and once you do that you are now ready to enter the unknown mall stores!

I say "unknown" because at night, it's like little elves come in and move all the racks around and set new displays and new aisles in which a wheelchair will have problems traversing. I know it's mean but whenever I see an aisle of clothes that is very narrow and almost impossible for a wheelchair to go down, I'll get a rolling head start and fly through the aisle as fast as I can, pulling clothes off the racks as I wheel through their meticulous rows!

This obviously doesn't make the store clerks happy, so I put on my poor paraplegic in a wheelchair look and say, "I'm sorry, I didn't know I was doing that!" ☺ But now that you've done all your shopping, and it's time to take all your treasures out to the car, you're at the mercy of the clerk you just got mad for pulling all the clothes off the rack! So be selective when you do the narrow aisle attack! ☺

88. Since the A.D.A. is there someplace you want to go but can't?

The A.D.A. was a monumental achievement for accessibility for the disabled, and just about every place I've wanted to go has been accessible. The one thing that I'd still love to do but can't is go into haunted houses with my wife. We've always like watching the ghost stories on TV, but the houses that they say are haunted are usually older and not accessible!

89. How do you feel when someone asks you if you need help?

I guess I'm different than most because I don't mind when others offer their assistance when I'm getting in or out of my car or just ask me if they can help me. The reason is, one day I just might need their help. So, I never get upset when they offer. I try to explain to them that I have a system or technique that I do that I can do faster and have the chair in the position I need it in to get in or out. When I do get upset is when they won't take no for an answer and persist in helping which ends up taking me twice as long. The chair ends up getting stuck or just doesn't work right because of something they've done to it.

90. Why do you usually refuse help?

As I said in the previous paragraph, there is usually a technique or system someone in a wheelchair gets into that works for them. They do things a certain way that make it routine and consistent so that each step is calculated and planned. When someone steps in to help, even though they have the very best intentions, it could be disastrous for the individual as they have disrupted their whole system. What they think is no big deal could be the start of a downward spiral of events just because they wanted to help. My advice is to honor their wishes, and if they refuse your help just say, "Okay, I was sure you could do it on your own but just checking to see if I could be of any assistance." That way if they do need your help, you've given them the opportunity to say, "Thanks, I really could use some help," if help is needed!

On the Lighter Side 9

Why catheterizing himself one day a young man was experiencing resistance while putting it in. In other words, it wasn't going in the way they usually do, and he was a little forceful and the catheter tore the inner lining of his penis. Now this is a tragic event, and you could have a hard time thinking this event would be funny. But while gripping his manhood and trying to figure out what to do, he had thoughts racing through his mind. He thought to himself, "I need to call 911, but how do I explain? There is no lesion or visible cut." Still gripping his manhood, he thought, "If the paramedics come, what kind of embarrassment would that cause? Could I bleed to death? That's just great!" He could imagine the front page of the paper, "Man bleeds to death due to hemorrhaging from his penis"! "What a way to die," he thought to himself!

He kept gripping and the bleeding started to slow. "Thank God," he thought and jumped into the shower and got washed off. The bleeding had just about completely stopped but he knew he had to get to the emergency room to be sure he was not bleeding internally. He was able to drive himself to the emergency room and you could only imagine how he had to explain to the girl at the emergency desk what his emergency was!

The doctor put in an indwelling catheter that has a small-balloon type end that (once it's inserted) they fill with saline to inflate the small balloon. This keeps the catheter in and allows the person to have an open flow anytime they need to urinate as it goes into a leg bag that is attached to the person's leg.

The doctor told him not to worry, that he did not permanently injure himself down there, but that it will heal on its own in a couple of days. The doctor said, "This is not common, but it will heal," and they both had a chuckle at the dilemma he had to go through in considering calling 911! But the doctor said if this were to happen again that he should call 911, because he could have lost too much blood and passed out while driving. As you well know, this would almost certainly cause an accident and possibly hurt someone else.

He agreed and just said that he prays that it will never happen again! Crisis averted, and he was relieved in more ways than one!

The Future

91. What would you do if a fire happened in your home?

This is a scary situation for anyone. The amount of time it takes to get transferred into my wheelchair and the time it takes to get out of my front door is very nerve-wracking. It's even more so when you're trying to save yourself, let alone trying to save anyone else.

Unfortunately, most individuals that are caught in a fire don't make it out unless they are helped by someone in the home or they are rescued by the firefighters. It's a good plan to have an escape route and who would be responsible for checking if the person in the chair got out.

At work we have fire drills and we have a selected person who volunteers to be the emergency help for a disabled person. Of course, that can all be thrown out the window if the designated person is not in the same location or is not in the building at the time. Our biggest problem would be debris, secondary to that would be the inability to get low to the ground to get what air we could breath.

Just the thought of it now makes my palms sweat. I just pray I'm never in that situation, because the possibilities would be grim. If you have a family member that is in a wheelchair it would be a good idea to make a master plan in case of a fire, tornado, hurricane, earthquake, or any other natural disaster you could think of. It is always better to be too prepared than not prepared at all!

92. How do you feel about medical marijuana?

For a lot of people medical marijuana can help those that are in extreme pain. Cannabis oil can help so many that I feel like it should be available to anyone that needs it for medical purposes. As far as those who smoke it, I'm still on the fence with that as I would hate it to be what they call a "gateway drug" to someone that gets relief from their pain only for it to lead to something stronger over time.

I feel for those people. They are the ones who I think would be prone to substance abuse because once they were able to alleviate some of their pain, they might look for something even stronger to achieve a longer and more profound euphoria. Then they would be creating a whole different problem in the pursuit of relief from their pain. I wouldn't blame them as I have seen some others go through extreme pain bad enough that they become desperate to try anything to get away it. I feel fortunate that I don't experience a lot of pain, most of my pain is tolerable and I've just learned how to deal with it.

93. How do you feel about stem cell treatments?

Oh boy do I have some feelings about this! As far as stem cells coming from a fetus, I'm pretty much against it. We all have our own stem cells that I think can be reinserted to help our bodies try to repair itself. The main thing I'm upset with is our inability to get things done in our great country. To have disabled individuals go to another country to get procedures done is just asinine if you ask me.

I was injured in 1990 and when I got hurt, they had not come out with the shot yet that was injected into the spinal cord to reduce swelling. It supposedly came out a couple months after my accident. But who's to say that I might not be walking today if the swelling had not choked off messages traveling through to my lower spine?

Regarding stem cells, scientists have already proven they work and not just for spinal cord-injured individuals, but for a multitude of different disabilities. When I first heard about stem cells it was about a year after my accident, but they've been around for years and have been the subject of a lot of studies and trials on mice.

Here's my thinking: do you know how many spinal cord injured individuals there are that would line up to be the first? Or who would line up to be the pioneers of getting a stem cell transplant with the hopes that they could be part of the cure? They have the technology, they have the resources, and I for one am sick and tired of hearing in another ten years they should have a cure! I call bullshit on that!

They can do it now, but the people who make money from the drugs, the supplies, the care, don't want to give that up!

I have been in the chair now going on thirty years, and I can honestly say that I've heard that statement every year since I've been paralyzed. "In ten more years!" Yeah, yeah, whatever! The biggest problem they would have would be who gets the treatments? Would it be the person who has been paralyzed for over twenty years? Hell no, it would be the newly injured that would get the treatments cause they have the greater possibility of having a successful result.

So, if you've been in a wheelchair as long as I have, I think we're shit out of luck! But here's my thought: what if they experimented on the ones that have been in the chair the longest? That way if they were to find a way to make them have good results wouldn't that just make it more advantageous to everyone else that was newly injured (or who have fewer years of injury?) I think so, so let's make it happen buttheads!

94. Would you get the operation?

That is a tough question, especially with the rant I just released in the prior question's answer. The reason is not that I would be scared, but that I'd have to put everyone's life on hold to see if Ken can get better. Work would be a problem. Needing time off to do rehabilitation, I'm not sure I could handle getting partially healed and not fully healed.

Whatever healing I did get would come with questions. Would it come with new pain due to non-usage of my muscles for so long? Would it cause me even more problems in the future? Could I handle the disappointment that it worked for others and not for me? How would I keep what I got and not lose more than I gained?

All these questions go through my mind thinking about this hypothetical question, so I guess the answer to it is ultimately no. Even if they came out with the cure tomorrow, I don't think I could put everyone I know through that, just to see what I could get back. I have a career and a family, and I can't just press pause and get an operation that might not work and could just bring me more problems. The ones that should get the operations to start with are the ones so unhappy with their lives and their disabilities that they would do anything not to live that way. I say pick the ones that are more than willing to take that chance and don't have a lot of family or responsibilities. But I for one would be eternally grateful to them as they could possibly help a lot of others with their choices. So, the whole thought of a cure is almost like a catch-22 situation: yeah it would be great unless it isn't great. So, again, to answer the question I'm saying, "No."

95. If you were to get the operation and everything went perfect what would be the first thing you would do?

Easy! I'd have sex and lots of it! ☺ The first

thing other than that would be to book a trip to a beautiful beach somewhere and take my wife, Vickie's, hand and walk with her on the beach. I then would go dancing and hold her tight like I was never going to let her go! There are so many things you think of that you miss due to being paralyzed. The feel of sand between your toes, the feel of grass when you walk across it, the sensation of putting your feet into a swimming pool or stream. Just little things that we often take for granted that we can feel are some of the best feelings that there are!

96. When did you start speaking?

I have always enjoyed talking and meeting people since I can remember (and a bit of showoff) so the combination of the two seemed like a good fit to me. After I was injured, I got a visit in the hospital by a few guys that had been in the chair for a while. That had one of the biggest impacts on me as I saw that yes there is life after a tragedy and that life does go on. One of the most memorable visits was from a T11 - T12 paraplegic by the name of Butch Trinca. He said, "Ken it's not what has happened to you, and it's not about what has happened in the past that really matters. It's what you do now and in the future!" He said, "You have a promising future ahead of you, and you'll amaze yourself and others at what you can and will do! Never limit yourself and try your best to forget the words 'I can't,' because you can!"

Well his words helped me, and I wanted to be

able to help others. So, whenever I get a call from a P.T. at the hospital to visit a newly injured person facing disabilities, I jump at the chance to hopefully give that individual the same help that those words gave me! So, I started visiting people in the hospital, and then I was invited to come up and speak to a group of people, and that's where it started as I felt like I had a message to share with others. What's this message? It's to create hope by showing these people that there are endless possibilities to life. Yes, there is tragedy. However, I think that some people who are struggling just need a little push to get them going in the right direction. I try to give them this push, to keep their minds open to different possibilities. Even though you have a plan and a direction for your life, it can be full of detours and roadblocks and you must be flexible enough to adjust your path or direction.

97. When you are speaking are you scared?

Ah stage fright, yes, it's real! But like I said before I don't mind being in front of others or speaking at any time, so it doesn't bother me that much. There are always butterflies before you go out and if you let the nerves get to you, they can cause mistakes. Recently I was doing a presentation in Virginia Beach, Virginia and I had a new power point that I was using, and it was going along pretty well, but when I was wrapping up the presentation, I always do the 4 C's.

The four C's are the C's that I live by and I reveal them to the audience in my closing remarks. The four C's are:

1. **Choice.** Everyone in this room can make a choice to change their direction or lane in life!
2. **Change.** Have the courage to make that change. You'll never know what you can do unless you take that chance.
3. **Chance.** Take a chance and try something you've never tried before; cause you'll never know if you can do it unless you challenge yourself.
4. **Challenge.** Challenge yourself to bigger and better things until you succeed, and once you succeed never stop challenging yourself cause that's what life is all about!

The audience was so great as it was attended by some high school kids and when I got to my second C, I accidentally skipped it and went onto the third C. When I got to the 4th C, I said, "And the fourth and final C," and they all stopped me as they were writing them all down and said, "Hey, that's only three C's!"

I had to chuckle and stop and tell them what the second C was that I left out, but to recover from my mistake I said, "Hey I was just checking to see if you all were still paying attention!"

98. How did you feel the first time you got a standing ovation?

I'll never forget it; I was speaking at the Hill Air Force Base Annual Disability Awards and had just wrapped up a great presentation. This was the first big one that my wife had attended and if you could have seen the look on both our faces as I was getting off the stage and the audience rises to their feet applauding, it was amazing! I was so honored to have been there and asked to present at this incredible event and was just blown away with the reaction of the crowd as I ended my presentation.

99. How do you feel about signing autographs?

That is amazing that someone would want my autograph. When I was on the Professional Bowlers Tour, I can remember the first time I was asked for it. I thought to myself, "Why do you want mine?" There are so many other bowlers out here that are so much better than me. This little boy looks up at me and said, "Because you're great and you're going to be the best!" Well, I didn't become the best but to be asked for my signature was truly an honor. So, when I sign my autograph on my books…again, I'm overwhelmed that someone would want my autograph. I try to sign every book that I sell if they want me to sign it, and I'm always honored to do it.

100. How much speaking do you want to do?

This is a hard question believe it or not. I have an incredible job and career working for the Utah State Office of Rehabilitation, and more specifically, the Utah Center for Assistive Technology. I love being able to help others who have unfortunately gotten into an accident or suffered a medical condition that changes their lives. The families and the individual are so lost when tragedy happens, and my heart goes out for them so much.

Being able to give them a glimmer of hope and just show them that you can still have a great life is my ultimate goal. Life isn't over, it has just changed. If you open your mind and your heart things can get better. So, I don't necessarily want to quit my day job.

However, if I got so busy that I had to choose between careers, I'd like to speak much more. I'd like to have a speaking career, but that remains to be seen and I just must trust in the Lord, and He will let me know my direction and my path to take. Also, I'd love to be able to speak in Hawaii so if you're reading this, and you know of any conferences out that way that would like me to come and address them, please call me and let me know! I'd love to come out and share my story with them. Other places I'd love to speak at would have to be Australia, England, Paris, Rio De Janeiro, Bora Bora, and the Bahamas, so if you have any contacts, hook me up!

101. Do you feel you're happier now than when you were able-bodied?

I can say that I wouldn't change anything in my life that has happened if it would change where I would be right now in this time and place. Am I happier than what I was? I would say yes? It's the people I met along my journey that have made the difference. First, I would go through all the heartbreak and pain I went through again just to meet my wife Vickie. She has made my life amazing. The support and love from my kids is irreplaceable and has absolutely completed my life. My career is the most rewarding in helping disabled individuals see that there is more to life and that they can go on. So, with the roller coaster ride of life I've been on (with its ups and downs and hair-raising curves) I'd have to say, yes, that my life is in a very happy place!

About the Author

Ken Reid is the bestselling author of *Choose A Lane*. He was injured in a car accident in 1990, which resulted in him becoming a T4 - T5 paraplegic. Utilizing a wheelchair for close to thirty years, he has gained a wealth of information and has written a book explaining some of the difficulties and techniques in dealing with life in a wheelchair. He's married and is the father of two grown children and is a grandfather. Ken was a professional bowler, World Cup bobsledder, and he works as an Assistive Technology Professional for the Utah Center for Assistive Technology (U.C.A.T.), which is part of the Department of Workforce Services (DWS Rehabilitation) in the great state of Utah.